DRAMATIS PERSONÆ

SIMO,[1] an aged Athenian.
PAMPHILUS,[2] son of Simo.
SOSIA,[3] freedman of Simo.
CHREMES,[4] an aged Athenian.
CHARINUS,[5] a young Athenian, in love with Philumena.
CRITO,[6] a native of Andros.
DAVUS,[7] servant of Simo.
DROMO,[8] servant of Simo.
BYRRHIA,[9] servant of Charinus.
GLYCERIUM,[10] a young woman beloved by Pamphilus.
MYSIS,[11] her maid-servant.
LESBIA,[12] a midwife.

SCENE:—Athens; before the houses of Simo and Glycerium.

THE SUBJECT

Chremes and Phania were brothers, citizens of Athens. Chremes going to Asia, leaves his daughter, Pasibula, in the care of his brother Phania, who, afterward setting sail with Pasibula for Asia, is wrecked off the Isle of Andros. Escaping with their lives, they are kindly received by a native of the island; and Phania soon afterward dies there. The Andrian changes the name of the girl to Glycerium, and brings her up, as his own child, with his daughter Chrysis. On his death, Chrysis and Glycerium sail for Athens to seek their fortune there. Chrysis being admired by several Athenian youths, Pamphilus, the son of Simo, an opulent citizen, chances to see Glycerium, and falls violently in love with her. She afterward becomes pregnant by him, on which he makes her a promise of marriage. In the mean time, Chremes, who is now living at Athens, and is ignorant of the fate of Pasibula, agrees with Simo, the father of Pamphilus, to give Philumena, another daughter, in marriage to Pamphilus. While these arrangements are being made, Chrysis dies; on which Simo accidentally discovers his son's connection with Glycerium. Chremes, also coming to hear of it, declines the match, having no idea that Glycerium is really his own daughter. Simo, however, in order to test his son's feelings, resolves to pretend that the marriage-day is fixed. Meeting Pamphilus in the town, he desires him to go home and prepare for the wedding, which is to take place immediately. In his perplexity, the youth has recourse to his servant Davus, who, having heard of the refusal of Chremes, suspects the design of Simo. At this conjuncture, Charinus, a friend of Pamphilus, who is enamored of Philumena, but has been rejected by her father, entreats Pamphilus to put off the marriage, for at least a few days. Disclosing his own aversion to the match, Pamphilus readily engages to do this. In order the more effectually to break it off, Davus advises Pamphilus to pretend a readiness to comply with his father's wishes, supposing that of course Chremes will steadily persist in his refusal. Pamphilus does as he is advised, on which Simo again applies to Chremes, who, after some entreaty, gives his consent. Just at this conjuncture, Glycerium is delivered of a son; and by the advice of Davus, it is laid before the door of Simo's house. Chremes happening to see it there, and ascertaining that Pamphilus is its father, again refuses to give him his daughter. At this moment, Crito, a native of Andros, arrives, who, being a relative of Chrysis, has come to Athens to look after her property. Through him,

Chremes discovers that Glycerium is no other than his long-lost daughter, Pasibula; on which he consents to her immediate marriage with Pamphilus, who promises Charinus that he will use his best endeavors to obtain for him the hand of Philumena.

THE TITLE OF THE PLAY

Performed at the Megalensian Games;[13] M. Fulvius and M. Glabrio being Curule Ædiles.[14] Ambivius Turpio and Lucius Atilius Prænestinus[15] performed it. Flaccus, the freedman of Claudius,[16] composed the music, to a pair of treble flutes and bass flutes[17] alternately. And it is entirely Grecian.[18] Published—M. Marcellus and Cneius Sulpicius being Consuls.[19]

ANDRIA; THE FAIR ANDRIAN

THE SUMMARY OF C. SULPITIUS APOLLINARIS

Pamphilus seduces Glycerium, wrongfully supposed to be a sister of a Courtesan, an Andrian by birth; and she having become pregnant, he gives his word that she shall be his wife; but his father has engaged for him another, the daughter of Chremes; and when he discovers the intrigue he pretends that the nuptials are about to take place, desiring to learn what intentions his son may have. By the advice of Davus, Pamphilus does not resist; but Chremes, as soon as he has seen the little child born of Glycerium, breaks off the match, and declines him for a son-in-law. Afterward, this Glycerium, unexpectedly discovered to be his own daughter, he bestows as a wife on Pamphilus, the other on Charinus.

THE PROLOGUE

The poet, when first he applied his mind to writing, thought that the only duty which devolved on him was, that the Plays he should compose might please the public. But he perceives that it has fallen out entirely otherwise; for he is wasting his labor in writing Prologues, not for the purpose of relating the plot, but to answer the slanders of a malevolent old Poet.[20] Now I beseech you, give your attention to the thing which they impute as a fault. Menander composed the Andrian[21] and the Perinthian.[22] He who knows either of them well, will know them both; they are in plot not very different, and yet they have been composed in different language and style. What suited, he confesses he has transferred into the Andrian from the Perinthian, and has employed them as his own. These parties censure this proceeding; and on this point they differ from him, that Plays ought not to be mixed up together. By being thus knowing, do they not show that they know nothing at all? For while they are censuring him, they are censuring Nævius, Plautus, and Ennius,[23] whom our Poet has for his precedents; whose carelessness he prefers to emulate, rather than the mystifying carefulness[24] of those parties. Therefore, I advise them to be quiet in future, and to cease to slander; that they may not be made acquainted with their own misdeeds. Be well disposed, then; attend with unbiased mind, and consider the matter, that you may determine what hope is left; whether the Plays which he shall in future compose anew, are to be witnessed, or are rather to be driven off the stage.

SCENE I

Enter **SIMO** and **SOSIA**, followed by **SERVANTS** carrying provisions.

SIMO [To the **SERVANTS**]
Do you carry those things away in-doors; begone.
[Beckoning to **SOSIA**]
Sosia, just step here; I want a few words with you.

SOSIA
Consider it as said; that these things are to be taken care of, I suppose.[25]

SIMO
No, it's another matter.

SOSIA
What is there that my ability can effect for you more than this?

SIMO
There's no need of that ability in the matter which I have in hand; but of those qualities which I have ever known as existing in you, fidelity and secrecy.

SOSIA
I await your will.

SIMO
Since I purchased you, you know that, from a little child, your servitude with me has always been easy and light. From a slave I made you my freedman;[26] for this reason, because you served me with readiness. The greatest recompense that I possessed, I bestowed upon you.

SOSIA
I bear it in mind.

SIMO
I am not changed.

SOSIA
If I have done or am doing aught that is pleasing to you, Simo, I am glad that it has been done; and that the same has been gratifying to you, I consider sufficient thanks. But this is a cause of uneasiness to me; for the recital is, as it were, a censure[27] to one forgetful of a kindness. But tell me, in one word, what it is that you want with me.

SIMO

I'll do so. In the first place, in this affair I give you notice: this, which you suppose to be such, is not a real marriage.

SOSIA
Why do you pretend it then?

SIMO
You shall hear all the matter from the beginning; by that means you'll be acquainted with both my son's mode of life and my own design, and what I want you to do in this affair. For after he had passed youthfulness,[28] Sosia, and had obtained free scope of living, (for before, how could you know or understand his disposition, while youthful age, fear, and a master[29] were checking him?)—

SOSIA
That's true.

SIMO
What all young men, for the most part, do,—devote their attention to some particular pursuit, either to training horses or dogs for hunting, or to the philosophers;[30] in not one of these did he engage in particular beyond the rest, and yet in all of them in a moderate degree. I was pleased.

SOSIA
Not without reason; for this I deem in life to be especially advantageous; that one do nothing to excess.[31]

SIMO
Such was his mode of life; readily to bear and to comply with all; with whomsoever he was in company, to them to resign himself; to devote himself to their pursuits; at variance with no one; never preferring himself to them. Thus most readily you may acquire praise without envy, and gain friends.

SOSIA
He has wisely laid down his rule of life; for in these days obsequiousness begets friends; sincerity, dislike.

SIMO
Meanwhile, three years ago,[32] a certain woman from Andros removed hither into this neighborhood, driven by poverty and the neglect of her relations, of surpassing beauty and in the bloom of youth.

SOSIA
Ah! I'm afraid that this Andrian will bring some mischief.

SIMO
At first, in a modest way, she passed her life with thriftiness and in hardship, seeking a livelihood with her wool and loom. But after an admirer made advances, promising her a recompense, first one and then another; as the disposition of all mankind has a downward tendency from industry toward pleasure, she accepted their proposals, and then began to trade upon her beauty. Those who then were her admirers, by chance, as it often happens, took my son thither that he might be in their company. Forthwith I said to myself, "He is surely caught; he is smitten."[33] In the morning I used to observe their servant-boys coming or going away; I used to make inquiry, "Here, my lad, tell me, will you, who had Chrysis yesterday?" for that was the name of the Andrian.

Andria (The Girl from Andros) by Terence

A Translation by Henry Thomas Riley

Publius Terentius Afer is better known to us as the Roman playwright, Terence.

Much of his life, especially the early part, is either unknown or has conflicting sources and accounts.

His birth date is said to be either 185 BC or a decade earlier: 195 BC. His place of birth is variously listed as in, or, near Carthage, or, in Greek Italy to a woman taken to Carthage as a slave. It is suggested that he lived in the territory of the Libyan tribe that the Romans called Afri, near Carthage, before being brought to Rome as a slave. Probability suggests that it was there, in North Africa, several decades after the destruction of Carthage by the Romans in 146 BC, at the end of the Punic Wars, that Terence spent his early years.

One reliable fact is that he was sold to P. Terentius Lucanus, a Roman senator, who had him educated and, impressed by his literary talents, freed him.

These writing talents were to ensure his legacy as a playwright down through the millennia. His comedies, partially adapted from Greek plays of the late phases of Attic Comedy, were performed for the first time around 170–160 BC. All six of the plays he has known to have written have survived.

Indeed, thanks to his simple conversational Latin, which was both entertaining and direct, Terence's works were heavily used by monasteries and convents during the Middle Ages and The Renaissance. Scribes often learned Latin through the copious copying of Terence's texts. Priests and nuns often learned to speak Latin through re-enactment of Terence's plays. Although his plays often dealt with pagan material, the quality and distinction of his language promoted the copying and preserving of his text by the church. This preservation enabled his work to influence a wide spectrum of later Western drama.

When he was 25 (or 35 depending on which year of birth you ascribe too), Terence travelled to Greece but never returned. It has long been assumed that he died at some point during the journey.

Of his own family nothing is known, except that he fathered a daughter and left a small but valuable estate just outside Rome.

His most famous quotation reads: "Homo sum, humani nihil a me alienum puto", or "I am human, and I think nothing human is alien to me."

Index of Contents

[Touching **SOSIA** on the arm.

SOSIA
I understand.

SIMO
Phædrus, or Clinias, or Niceratus, they used to say; for these three then loved her at the same time. "Well now, what did Pamphilus do?" "What? He gave his contribution;[34] he took part in the dinner." Just so on another day I made inquiry, but I discovered nothing whatever that affected Pamphilus. In fact, I thought him sufficiently proved, and a great pattern of continence; for he who is brought into contact with dispositions of that sort, and his feelings are not aroused even under such circumstances, you may be sure that he is already capable of undertaking the governance of his own life. This pleased me, and every body with one voice began to say all kinds of flattering things, and to extol my good fortune, in having a son endowed with such a disposition. What need is there of talking? Chremes, influenced by this report, came to me of his own accord, to offer his only daughter as a wife to my son, with a very large portion. It pleased me; I betrothed him; this was the day appointed for the nuptials.

SOSIA
What then stands in the way? Why should they not take place?

SIMO
You shall hear. In about a few days after these things had been agreed on, Chrysis, this neighbor, dies.

SOSIA
Bravo! You've made me happy. I was afraid for him on account of Chrysis.

SIMO
Then my son was often there, with those who had admired Chrysis; with them he took charge of the funeral; sorrowful, in the mean time, he sometimes wept with them in condolence. Then that pleased me. Thus I reflected: "He by reason of this slight intimacy takes her death so much to heart; what if he himself had wooed her? What will he do for me his father?" All these things I took to be the duties of a humane disposition and of tender feelings. Why do I detain you with many words? Even I myself,[35] for his sake, went forth to the funeral, as yet suspecting no harm.

SOSIA
Ha! what is this?

SIMO
You shall know. She is brought out; we proceed. In the mean time, among the females who were there present, I saw by chance one young woman of beauteous form.

SOSIA
Very likely.

SIMO
And of countenance, Sosia, so modest, so charming, that nothing could surpass. As she appeared to me to lament beyond the rest, and as she was of a figure handsome and genteel beyond the other women, I

approached the female attendants;[36] I inquired who she was. They said that she was the sister of Chrysis. It instantly struck my mind: "Ay, ay, this is it; hence those tears, hence that sympathy."

SOSIA

How I dread what you are coming to!

SIMO

The funeral procession meanwhile advances; we follow; we come to the burying-place.[37] She is placed upon the pile; they weep. In the mean time, this sister, whom I mentioned, approached the flames too incautiously, with considerable danger. There, at that moment, Pamphilus, in his extreme alarm, discovers his well-dissembled and long-hidden passion; he runs up, clasps the damsel by the waist. "My Glycerium," says he, "what are you doing? Why are you going to destroy yourself?" Then she, so that you might easily recognize their habitual attachment, weeping, threw herself back upon him—how affectionately!

SOSIA

What do you say?

SIMO

I returned thence in anger, and hurt at heart: and yet there was not sufficient ground for reproving him. He might say; "What have I done? How have I deserved this, or offended, father? She who wished to throw herself into the flames, I prevented; I saved her." The defense is a reasonable one.

SOSIA

You judge aright; for if you censure him who has assisted to preserve life, what are you to do to him who causes loss or misfortune to it?

SIMO

Chremes comes to me next day, exclaiming: "Disgraceful conduct!"—that he had ascertained that Pamphilus was keeping this foreign woman as a wife. I steadfastly denied that to be the fact. He insisted that it was the fact. In short, I then left him refusing to bestow his daughter.

SOSIA

Did not you then reprove your son?

SIMO

Not even this was a cause sufficiently strong for censuring him.

SOSIA

How so? Tell me.

SIMO

"You yourself, father," he might say, "have prescribed a limit to these proceedings. The time is near, when I must live according to the humor of another; meanwhile, for the present allow me to live according to my own."

SOSIA

What room for reproving him, then, is there left?

SIMO

If on account of his amour he shall decline to take a wife, that, in the first place, is an offense on his part to be censured. And now for this am I using my endeavors, that, by means of the pretended marriage, there may be real ground for rebuking him, if he should refuse; at the same time, that if that rascal Davus has any scheme, he may exhaust it now, while his knaveries can do no harm: who, I do believe, with hands, feet, and all his might, will do every thing; and more for this, no doubt, that he may do me an ill turn, than to oblige my son.

SOSIA

For what reason?

SIMO

Do you ask? Bad heart, bad disposition. Whom, however, if I do detect—But what need is there of talking? If it should turn out, as I wish, that there is no delay on the part of Pamphilus, Chremes remains to be prevailed upon by me; and I do hope that all will go well. Now it's your duty to pretend these nuptials cleverly, to terrify Davus; and watch my son, what he's about, what schemes he is planning with him.

SOSIA

'Tis enough; I'll take care; now let's go in-doors.

SIMO

You go first; I'll follow.

[**SOSIA** goes into the house of **SIMO**.

SIMO [To himself]

There's no doubt but that my son doesn't wish for a wife; so alarmed did I perceive Davus to be just now, when he heard that there was going to be a marriage. But the very man is coming out of the house.

[Stands aside.

SCENE II

Enter **DAVUS** from the house of **SIMO**.

DAVUS [Aloud to himself]

I was wondering if this matter was to go off thus; and was continually dreading where my master's good humor would end; for, after he had heard that a wife would not be given to his son, he never uttered a word to any one of us, or took it amiss.

SIMO [Apart, overhearing him]

But now he'll do so: and that, I fancy, not without heavy cost to you.

DAVUS [To himself]

He meant this, that we, thus unsuspecting, should be led away by delusive joy; that now in hope, all fear being removed, we might during our supineness be surprised, so that there might be no time for planning a rupture of the marriage. How clever!

SIMO [Apart]

The villain! what does he say?

DAVUS [Overhearing him, to himself]

It's my master, and I didn't see him.

SIMO

Davus.

DAVUS

Well, what is it?

SIMO

Just step this way to me.

DAVUS [To himself]

What does he want?

SIMO

What are you saying?

DAVUS

About what?

SIMO

Do you ask the question? There's a report that my son's in love.

DAVUS

The public troubles itself about that,[38] of course.

SIMO

Will you attend to this, or not?

DAVUS

Certainly, I will, to that.

SIMO

But for me to inquire now into these matters, were the part of a severe father. For what he has done hitherto, doesn't concern me at all. So long as his time of life prompted to that course, I allowed him to indulge his inclination: now this day brings on another mode of life, demands other habits. From this time forward, I do request, or if it is reasonable, I do entreat you, Davus, that he may now return to the right path.

DAVUS [Aside]
What can this mean?

SIMO
All who are intriguing take it ill to have a wife given them.

DAVUS
So they say.

SIMO
And if any one has adopted a bad instructor in that course, he generally urges the enfeebled mind to pursuits still more unbecoming.

DAVUS
'faith, I do not comprehend.

SIMO
No? Ha—

DAVUS
No—I am Davus, not Œdipus.[39]

SIMO
Of course then, you wish me to speak plainly in what further I have to say.

DAVUS
Certainly, by all means.

SIMO
If I this day find out that you are attempting any trickery about this marriage, to the end that it may not take place; or are desirous that in this matter it should be proved how knowing you are; I'll hand you over, Davus, beaten with stripes, to the mill,[40] even to your dying day, upon this condition and pledge, that if ever I release you, I shall grind in your place. Now, do you understand this? Or not yet even this?

DAVUS
Yes, perfectly: you have now spoken so plainly upon the subject, you have not used the least circumlocution.

SIMO
In any thing would I more willingly allow myself to be imposed upon than in this matter.

DAVUS
Fair words, I entreat.

SIMO
You are ridiculing me: you don't at all deceive me. I give you warning, don't act rashly, and don't say you were not warned. Take care.

[Shaking his stick, goes into the house.

SCENE III

DAVUS alone.

DAVUS [To himself]
Assuredly, Davus, there's no room for slothfulness or inactivity, so far as I've just now ascertained the old man's mind about the marriage; which if it is not provided against by cunning, will be bringing either myself or my master to ruin. What to do, I am not determined; whether I should assist Pamphilus or obey the old man. If I desert the former, I fear for his life; if I assist him, I dread the other's threats, on whom it will be a difficult matter to impose. In the first place, he has now found out about this amour; with hostile feelings he watches me, lest I should be devising some trickery against the marriage. If he discovers it, I'm undone; or even if he chooses to allege any pretext, whether rightfully or wrongfully, he will consign me headlong to the mill. To these evils this one is besides added for me. This Andrian, whether she is his wife, or whether his mistress, is pregnant by Pamphilus. It is worth while to hear their effrontery; for it is an undertaking worthy of those in their dotage, not of those who dote in love;[41] whatever she shall bring forth, they have resolved to rear;[42] and they are now contriving among themselves a certain scheme, that she is a citizen of Attica. There was formerly a certain old man of this place, a merchant; he was shipwrecked off the Isle of Andros; he died. They say that there, the father of Chrysis, on that occasion, sheltered this girl, thrown on shore, an orphan, a little child. What nonsense! To myself at least it isn't very probable; the fiction pleases them, however. But Mysis is coming out of the house. Now I'll betake myself hence to the Forum,[43] that I may meet with Pamphilus, lest his father should take him by surprise about this matter.

[Exit.

SCENE IV

Enter **MYSIS** from the house of **GLYCERIUM**.

MYSIS [Speaking at the door to **ARCHYLIS** within]
I've heard you already, Archylis; you request Lesbia to be fetched. Really, upon my faith, she is a wine-bibbing[44] and a rash woman, and not sufficiently trustworthy for you to commit to her care a female at her first delivery; is she still to be brought?

[She receives an answer from within, and comes forward.

Do look at the inconsiderateness of the old woman; because she is her pot-companion. Ye Gods, I do entreat you, give her ease in her delivery, and to that woman an opportunity of making her mistakes elsewhere in preference. But why do I see Pamphilus so out of spirits? I fear what it may be. I'll wait, that I may know whether this sorrow portends any disaster.

[Stands apart.

Enter **PAMPHILUS**, wringing his hands.

PAMPHILUS [To himself]
Is it humane to do or to devise this? Is this the duty of a father?

MYSIS [Apart]
What does this mean?

PAMPHILUS [To himself]
O, by our faith in the Gods! what is, if this is not, an indignity? He had resolved that he himself would give me a wife to-day; ought I not to have known this beforehand? Ought it not to have been mentioned previously?

MYSIS [Apart]
Wretched me! What language do I hear?

PAMPHILUS [To himself]
What does Chremes do? He who had declared that he would not intrust his daughter to me as a wife; because he himself sees me unchanged he has changed. Thus perversely does he lend his aid, that he may withdraw wretched me from Glycerium. If this is effected, I am utterly undone. That any man should be so unhappy in love, or so unfortunate as I am! Oh, faith of Gods and men! shall I by no device be able to escape this alliance with Chremes? In how many ways am I contemned, and held in scorn? Every thing done, and concluded! Alas! once rejected I am sought again; for what reason? Unless perhaps it is this, which I suspect it is: they are rearing some monster,[45] and as she can not be pushed off upon any one else, they have recourse to me.

MYSIS [Apart]
This language has terrified wretched me with apprehension.

PAMPHILUS [To himself]
But what am I to say about my father? Alas! that he should so thoughtlessly conclude an affair of such importance! Passing me in the Forum just now, he said, "Pamphilus, you must be married to-day: get ready; be off home." He seemed to me to say this: "Be off this instant, and go hang yourself." I was amazed; think you that I was able to utter a single word, or any excuse, even a frivolous, false, or lame one? I was speechless. But if any one were to ask me now what I would have done, if I had known this sooner, why, I would have done any thing rather than do this. But now, what course shall I first adopt? So many cares beset me, which rend my mind to pieces; love, sympathy for her, the worry of this marriage; then, respect for my father, who has ever, until now, with such an indulgent disposition, allowed me to do whatever was agreeable to my feelings. Ought I to oppose him? Ah me! I am in uncertainty what to do.

MYSIS [Apart]

I'm wretchedly afraid how this uncertainty is to terminate. But now there's an absolute necessity, either for him to speak to her, or for me to speak to him about her. While the mind is in suspense, it is swayed by a slight impulse one way or the other.

PAMPHILUS [Overhearing her]
Who is it speaking here?
[Seeing her]
Mysis? Good-morrow to you.

MYSIS
Oh! Good-morrow to you, Pamphilus.

PAMPHILUS
How is she?

MYSIS
Do you ask? She is oppressed with grief,[46] and on this account the poor thing is anxious, because some time ago the marriage was arranged for this day. Then, too, she fears this, that you may forsake her.

PAMPHILUS
Ha! could I attempt that? Could I suffer her, poor thing, to be deceived on my account? She, who has confided to me her affection, and her entire existence? She, whom I have held especially dear to my feelings as my wife? Shall I suffer her mind, well and chastely trained and tutored, to be overcome by poverty and corrupted? I will not do it.

MYSIS
I should have no fear if it rested with yourself alone; but whether you may be able to withstand compulsion—

PAMPHILUS
Do you deem me so cowardly, so utterly ungrateful, inhuman, and so brutish, that neither intimacy, nor affection, nor shame, can move or admonish me to keep faith?

MYSIS
This one thing I know, that she is deserving that you should not forget her.

PAMPHILUS
Forget her? Oh Mysis, Mysis, at this moment are those words of Chrysis concerning Glycerium written on my mind. Now at the point of death, she called me; I went to her; you had withdrawn; we were alone; she began: "My dear Pamphilus, you see her beauty and her youth; and it is not unknown to you to what extent both of these are now of use to her, in protecting both her chastity and her interests. By this right hand I do entreat you, and by your good Genius,[47] by your own fidelity, and by her bereft condition, do not withdraw yourself from her, or forsake her; if I have loved you as my own brother, or if she has always prized you above all others, or has been obedient to you in all things. You do I give to her as a husband, friend, protector, father. This property of mine do I intrust to you, and commit to your care." She placed her in my hands; that instant, death came upon her. I accepted her; having accepted, I will protect her.

MYSIS
So indeed I hope.

[Moving.

PAMPHILUS
But why are you leaving her?

MYSIS
I'm going to fetch the midwife.[48]

PAMPHILUS
Make all haste. And—do you hear?—take care, and not one word about the marriage, lest that too should add to her illness.

MYSIS
I understand.

[Exeunt **SEVERALLY**.

ACT THE SECOND

SCENE I

Enter **CHARINUS** and **BYRRHIA**.[49]

CHARINUS
How say you, Byrrhia? Is she to be given in marriage to Pamphilus to-day?

BYRRHIA
It is so.

CHARINUS
How do you know?

BYRRHIA
I heard it just now from Davus at the Forum.

CHARINUS
Woe unto wretched me! As, hitherto, until now, my mind has been racked amid hope and fear; so, since hope has been withdrawn, wearied with care, it sinks overwhelmed.

BYRRHIA
By my troth, Charinus, since that which you wish can not come to pass, prithee, do wish that which can.

CHARINUS
I wish for nothing else but Philumena.

BYRRHIA
Alas! How much better were it for you to endeavor to expel that passion from your mind, than to be saying that by which your desire is to no purpose still more inflamed.

CHARINUS
We all, when we are well, with ease give good advice to the sick. If you were in my situation, you would think otherwise.

BYRRHIA
Well, well, just as you like.

CHARINUS [Looking down the side scene]
But I see Pamphilus; I'm determined I'll try every thing before I despair.

BYRRHIA [Aside]
What does he mean?

CHARINUS
I will entreat his own self; I will supplicate him; I will disclose to him my love. I think that I shall prevail upon him to put off the marriage for some days at least; in the mean time, something will turn up, I trust.

BYRRHIA
That something is nothing.

CHARINUS
Byrrhia, how seems it to you? Shall I accost him?

BYRRHIA
Why not? Should you not prevail, that at least he may look upon you as a gallant ready provided for him, if he marries her.

CHARINUS
Away with you to perdition with that vile suggestion, you rascal!

SCENE II

Enter **PAMPHILUS**.

PAMPHILUS
I espy Charinus.
[Accosting him]
Good-morrow!

CHARINUS
O, good-morrow. Pamphilus, I'm come to you, seeking hope, safety, counsel, and assistance.

PAMPHILUS
I'faith, I have neither time for counsel, nor resources for assistance. But what's the matter now?

CHARINUS
To-day you are going to take a wife?

PAMPHILUS
So they say.

CHARINUS
Pamphilus, if you do that, you behold me this day for the last time.

PAMPHILUS
Why so?

CHARINUS
Ah me! I dread to tell it; prithee, do you tell it, Byrrhia.

BYRRHIA
I'll tell it.

PAMPHILUS
What is it?

BYRRHIA
He's in love with your betrothed.

PAMPHILUS
Assuredly he's not of my way of thinking. Come now, tell me, have you had any more to do with her, Charinus?

CHARINUS
Oh Pamphilus, nothing.

PAMPHILUS
How much I wish you had.

CHARINUS
Now, by our friendship and by my affection, I do beseech you, in the first place, not to marry her.

PAMPHILUS
For my own part I'll use my endeavors.

CHARINUS

But if that can not be, or if this marriage is agreeable to you—

PAMPHILUS
Agreeable to me?

CHARINUS
Put it off for some days at least, while I go elsewhere, that I may not be witness.

PAMPHILUS
Now listen, once for all: I think it, Charinus, to be by no means the part of an ingenuous man, when he confers nothing, to expect that it should be considered as an obligation on his part. I am more desirous to avoid this match, than you to gain it.

CHARINUS
You have restored me to life.

PAMPHILUS
Now, if you can do any thing, either you yourself, or Byrrhia here, manage, fabricate, invent, contrive some means, whereby she may be given to you; this I shall aim at, how she may not be given to me.

CHARINUS
I am satisfied.

PAMPHILUS
Most opportunely I perceive Davus, on whose advice I have depended.

CHARINUS [Turning to **BYRRHIA**]
But you, i'faith, tell me nothing,[50] except those things which there is no need for knowing.
[Pushing him away]
Get you gone from here.

BYRRHIA
Certainly I will, and with all my heart.

[Exit.

SCENE III

Enter **DAVUS** in haste.

DAVUS [Not seeing **PAMPHILUS** and **CHARINUS**]
Ye gracious Gods, what good news I bring! But where shall I find Pamphilus, that I may remove the apprehension in which he now is, and fill his mind with joy—?

CHARINUS [Apart to **PAMPHILUS**]
He's rejoiced about something, I don't know what.

PAMPHILUS [Apart]
It's of no consequence; he hasn't yet heard of these misfortunes.

DAVUS [To himself]
For I do believe now, if he has already heard that a marriage is prepared for him—

CHARINUS [Apart]
Don't you hear him?

DAVUS [To himself]
He is seeking me distractedly all the city over. But where shall I look for him? Or in which direction now first to betake me—

CHARINUS [Apart to **PAMPHILUS**]
Do you hesitate to accost him?

DAVUS [To himself]
I have it.

[Moving on.

PAMPHILUS
Davus, come here! Stop!

DAVUS
Who's the person that's—
[Turning round]
O Pamphilus, you are the very man I'm looking for. Well done, Charinus! both in the nick of time: I want you both.

CHARINUS
Davus, I'm undone!

DAVUS
Nay but, do hear this.

PAMPHILUS
I'm utterly ruined!

DAVUS
I know what you are afraid of.

CHARINUS
I'faith, my life indeed is really in danger.

DAVUS [To **CHARINUS**]
And what you are afraid of, I know.

PAMPHILUS

My marriage—

DAVUS

As if I did not know it?

PAMPHILUS

This day—

DAVUS

Why keep dinning me with it, when I know it all?
[To **PAMPHILUS**]
This are you afraid of, lest you should marry her; and you—
[To **CHARINUS**]
—lest you should not marry her.

CHARINUS

You understand the matter.

PAMPHILUS

That's the very thing.

DAVUS

And that very thing is in no danger; trust me for that.

PAMPHILUS

I do entreat you, release wretched me as soon as possible from this apprehension.

DAVUS

Well, then, I will release you; Chremes is not going to give you his daughter at present.

PAMPHILUS

How do you know?

DAVUS

You shall know. Your father just now laid hold of me; he said that a wife was to be given you to-day, and many other things as well, which just now I haven't time to relate. Hastening to you immediately, I ran on to the Forum that I might tell you these things. When I didn't find you, I ascended there to a high place.[51] I looked around; you were nowhere. There by chance I saw Byrrhia, his servant.
[Pointing to **CHARINUS**]
I inquired of him; he said he hadn't seen you. This puzzled me. I considered what I was to do. As I was returning in the mean time, a surmise from the circumstances themselves occurred to me: "How now,— a very small amount of good cheer; he out of spirits; a marriage all of a sudden; these things don't agree."

PAMPHILUS

But to what purpose this?

DAVUS
I forthwith betook myself to the house of Chremes. When I arrived there—stillness before the door;[52] then I was pleased at that.

CHARINUS
You say well.

PAMPHILUS
Proceed.

DAVUS
I stopped there. In the mean time I saw no one going in, no one going out; no matron at the house,[53] no preparation, no bustle. I drew near; looked in—

PAMPHILUS
I understand; a considerable indication.

DAVUS
Do these things seem to accord with a wedding?

PAMPHILUS
I think not, Davus.

DAVUS
Think, do you say? You don't view it rightly; the thing is certain. Besides, coming away from there I saw the servant-boy of Chremes carrying some vegetables and little fishes, an obol's worth,[54] for the old man's dinner.

CHARINUS
This day, Davus, have I been delivered by your means.

DAVUS
And yet not at all.

CHARINUS
Why so? Surely he will not give her to him, after all this.

[Pointing to **PAMPHILUS**.

DAVUS
You silly fellow! as though it were a necessary consequence that if he doesn't give her to him you should marry her: unless, indeed, you look about you; unless you entreat and make court to the old man's friends.

CHARINUS
You advise well. I'll go; although, upon my faith, this hope has often eluded me already. Farewell!

[Exit.

PAMPHILUS and **DAVUS**.

PAMPHILUS
What then does my father mean? Why does he thus make pretense?

DAVUS
I'll tell you. If now he were angry with you, because Chremes will not give you a wife, he would seem to himself to be unjust, and that not without reason, before he has ascertained your feelings as to the marriage, how they are disposed. But if you refuse to marry her, in that case he will transfer the blame to you; then such disturbances will arise.

PAMPHILUS
I will submit to any thing from him.

DAVUS
He is your father, Pamphilus. It is a difficult matter. Besides, this woman is defenseless. No sooner said than done; he will find some pretext for driving her away from the city.

PAMPHILUS
Driving her away?

DAVUS
Aye, and quickly too.

PAMPHILUS
Tell me then, Davus, what am I to do?

DAVUS
Say that you will marry her.

PAMPHILUS [Starting]
Ha!

DAVUS
What's the matter?

PAMPHILUS
What, am I to say so?

DAVUS
Why not?

PAMPHILUS

Never will I do it.

DAVUS

Don't say so.

PAMPHILUS

Don't attempt to persuade me.

DAVUS

Consider what will be the result of it.

PAMPHILUS

That I shall be deprived of the one, and fixed with the other.

DAVUS

Not so. In fact, I think it will be thus: Your father will say: "I wish you to marry a wife to-day." You reply: "I'll marry her." Tell me, how can he raise a quarrel with you? Thus you will cause all the plans which are now arranged by him to be disarranged, without any danger; for this is not to be doubted, that Chremes will not give you his daughter. Therefore do not hesitate in those measures which you are taking, on this account, lest he should change his sentiments. Tell your father that you consent; so that although he may desire it, he may not be able to be angry at you with reason. For that which you rely on, I will easily refute; "No one," you think, "will give a wife to a person of these habits." But he will find a beggar for you, rather than allow you to be corrupted by a mistress. If, however, he shall believe that you bear it with a contented mind, you will render him indifferent; at his leisure he will look out for another wife for you; in the mean time something lucky may turn up.

PAMPHILUS

Do you think so?

DAVUS

It really is not a matter of doubt.

PAMPHILUS

Consider to what you are persuading me.

DAVUS

Nay, but do be quiet.

PAMPHILUS

Well, I'll say it; but, that he mayn't come to know that she has had a child by me, is a thing to be guarded against; for I have promised to bring it up.

DAVUS

Oh, piece of effrontery.

PAMPHILUS

She entreated me that I would give her this pledge, by which she might be sure she should not be deserted.

DAVUS
It shall be attended to; but your father's coming. Take care that he doesn't perceive that you are out of spirits.

SCENE V

Enter **SIMO**, at a distance.

SIMO [Apart to himself]
I've come back to see what they are about, or what scheme they are hatching.

DAVUS [To **PAMPHILUS**]
He has no doubt at present but that you'll refuse to marry. Having considered his course, he's come from a retired spot somewhere or other; he hopes that he has framed a speech by which to disconcert you; do you take care, then, to be yourself.

PAMPHILUS
If I am only able, Davus.

DAVUS
Trust me for that, Pamphilus, I tell you; your father will never this day exchange a single word with you, if you say that you will marry.

SCENE VI

Enter **BYRRHIA**, unperceived, at a distance behind **SIMO**.

BYRRHIA [Apart to himself]
My master has ordered me, leaving my business, to keep an eye on Pamphilus to-day, what he is doing with regard to the marriage. I was to learn it; for that reason, I have now followed him[55]—
[Pointing to **SIMO**]
—as he came hither. Himself, as well, I see standing with Davus close at hand; I'll note this.

SIMO [Apart to himself]
I see that both of them are here.

DAVUS [In a low voice to **PAMPHILUS**]
Now then, be on your guard.

SIMO
Pamphilus!

DAVUS [In a low voice]
Look round at him as though taken unawares.

PAMPHILUS [Turning round sharply]
What, my father!

DAVUS [In a low voice]
Capital!

SIMO
I wish you to marry a wife to-day, as I was saying.

BYRRHIA [Apart]
Now I'm in dread for our side, as to what he will answer.

PAMPHILUS
Neither in that nor in any thing else shall you ever find any hesitation in me.

BYRRHIA [Apart]
Hah!

DAVUS [In a low voice to **PAMPHILUS**]
He is struck dumb.

BYRRHIA [Apart]
What a speech!

SIMO
You act as becomes you, when that which I ask I obtain with a good grace.

DAVUS [Aside to **PAMPHILUS**]
Am I right?

BYRRHIA
My master, so far as I learn, has missed his wife.

SIMO
Now, then, go in-doors, that you mayn't be causing delay when you are wanted.

PAMPHILUS
I'll go.

[Goes into the house.

BYRRHIA [Apart]
Is there, in no case, putting trust in any man? That is a true proverb which is wont to be commonly quoted, that "all had rather it to be well for themselves than for another." I remember noticing, when I

saw her, that she was a young woman of handsome figure; wherefore I am the more disposed to excuse Pamphilus, if he has preferred that he himself, rather than the other, should embrace her in his slumbers. I'll carry back these tidings, that, in return for this evil he may inflict evil upon me.[56]

[Exit.

SCENE VII

SIMO and **DAVUS**.

DAVUS [Aside, coming away from the door of the house]
He now supposes that I'm bringing some trick to bear against him, and that on that account I've remained here.

SIMO
What does he say, Davus?[57]

DAVUS
Just as much as nothing.[58]

SIMO
What, nothing? Eh?

DAVUS
Nothing at all.

SIMO
And yet I certainly was expecting something.

DAVUS
It has turned out contrary to your expectations.
[Aside]
I perceive it; this vexes the man.

SIMO
Are you able to tell me the truth?

DAVUS
I? Nothing more easy.

SIMO
Is this marriage at all disagreeable to him, on account of his intimacy with this foreign woman?

DAVUS
No, faith; or if at all, it is a two or three days' annoyance this—you understand. It will then cease. Moreover, he himself has thought over this matter in a proper way.

SIMO

I commend him.

DAVUS

While it was allowed him, and while his years prompted him, he intrigued; even then it was secretly. He took precaution that that circumstance should never be a cause of disgrace to him, as behooves a man of principle; now that he must have a wife, he has set his mind upon a wife.

SIMO

He seemed to me to be somewhat melancholy in a slight degree.

DAVUS

Not at all on account of her, but there's something he blames you for.

SIMO

What is it, pray?

DAVUS

It's a childish thing.

SIMO

What is it?

DAVUS

Nothing at all.

SIMO

Nay but, tell me what it is.

DAVUS

He says that you are making too sparing preparations.

SIMO

What, I?

DAVUS

You.—He says that there has hardly been fare provided to the amount of ten drachmæ.[59]—"Does he seem to be bestowing a wife on his son? Which one now, in preference, of my companions shall I invite to the dinner?" And, it must be owned, you really are providing too parsimoniously—I do not commend you.

SIMO

Hold your tongue.

DAVUS [Aside]

I've touched him up.

SIMO
I'll see that these things are properly done.

[**DAVUS** goes into the house.

What's the meaning of this? What does this old rogue mean? But if there's any knavery here, why, he's sure to be the source of the mischief.

[Goes into his house.

Enter **SIMO** and **DAVUS** from the house of the former. **MYSIS** and **LESBIA** are coming toward the house of **GLYCERIUM**.

MYSIS [Not seeing **SIMO** and **DAVUS**]
Upon my faith, the fact is really as you mentioned, Lesbia, you can hardly find a man constant to a woman.

SIMO [Apart to **DAVUS**]
This maid-servant comes from the Andrian.

DAVUS [Apart to **SIMO**]
What do you say?

SIMO [Apart to **DAVUS**]
It is so.

MYSIS
But this Pamphilas—

SIMO [Apart to **DAVUS**]
What is she saying?

MYSIS
Has proved his constancy.

SIMO [Apart]
Hah!

DAVUS [Apart to himself]
I wish that either he were deaf, or she struck dumb.

MYSIS

For the child she brings forth, he has ordered to be brought up.

SIMO [Apart]
O Jupiter! What do I hear! It's all over, if indeed this woman speaks the truth.

LESBIA
You mention a good disposition on the part of the young man.

MYSIS
A most excellent one. But follow me in-doors, that you mayn't keep her waiting.

LESBIA
I'll follow.

[**MYSIS** and **LESBIA** go into **GLYCERIUM'S** house.

SCENE II

SIMO and **DAVUS**.

DAVUS [Aside]
What remedy now shall I find for this mishap?

SIMO [To himself aloud]
What does this mean? Is he so infatuated? The child of a foreign woman? Now I understand; ah! scarcely even at last, in my stupidity, have I found it out.

DAVUS [Aside to himself]
What does he say he has found out?

SIMO [Aside]
This piece of knavery is being now for the first time palmed upon me by this fellow; they are pretending that she's in labor, in order that they may alarm Chremes.

GLYCERIUM [Exclaiming from within her house]
Juno Lucina,[60] grant me thine aid, save me, I do entreat thee!

SIMO
Whew! so sudden? What nonsense! As soon as she has heard that I'm standing before the door, she makes all haste. These incidents, Davus, have not been quite happily adapted by you as to the points of time.

DAVUS
By me?

SIMO

Are your scholars forgetful?[61]

DAVUS
I don't know what you are talking about.

SIMO [Aside]
If he at the real marriage of my son had taken me off my guard, what sport he would have made of me. Now it is at his own risk; I'm sailing in harbor.

SCENE III

Re-enter **LESBIA** from the house of **GLYCERIUM**.

LESBIA [Speaking to **ARCHYLIS** at the door, and not seeing **SIMO** and **DAVUS**]
As yet, Archylis, all the customary symptoms which ought to exist toward recovery, I perceive in her. Now, in the first place, take care and let her bathe;[62] then, after that, what I ordered to be given her to drink, and as much as I prescribed, do you administer: presently I will return hither.
[To herself aloud]
By all that's holy, a fine boy has been born to Pamphilus. I pray the Gods that he may survive, since the father himself is of a good disposition, and since he has hesitated to do an injustice to this most excellent young woman.
[Exit.

SCENE IV

SIMO and **DAVUS**.

SIMO
Even this, who is there that knows you that would not believe that it originated in you?

DAVUS
Why, what is this?

SIMO
She didn't order in their presence what was requisite to be done for the woman lying in; but after she has come out, she bawls from the street to those who are in the house. O Davus, am I thus trifled with by you? Or pray, do I seem to you so very well suited to be thus openly imposed upon by your tricks? At all events it should have been with precaution; that at least I might have seemed to be feared if I should detect it.

DAVUS [Aside]
Assuredly, upon my faith, it's he that's now deceiving himself, not I.

SIMO

I gave you warning, I forbade you with threats to do it. Have you been awed? What has it availed? Am I to believe you now in this, that this woman has had a child by Pamphilus?

DAVUS [Aside]
I understand where he's mistaken; and I see what I must do.

SIMO
Why are you silent?

DAVUS
What would you believe? As though word had not been brought you that thus it would happen.

SIMO
Any word brought to me?

DAVUS
Come now, did you of your own accord perceive that this was counterfeited?

SIMO
I am being trifled with.

DAVUS
Word has been brought you; for otherwise how could this suspicion have occurred to you?

SIMO
How? Because I knew you.

DAVUS
As though you meant to say that this has been done by my contrivance.

SIMO
Why, I'm sure of it, to a certainty.

DAVUS
Not yet even do you know me sufficiently, Simo, what sort of person I am.

SIMO
I, not know you!

DAVUS
But if I begin to tell you any thing, at once you think that deceit is being practiced upon you in guile; therefore, upon my faith, I don't dare now even to whisper.

SIMO
This one thing I am sure of, that no person has been delivered here.

[Pointing to **GLYCERIUM'S** house.

DAVUS

You have discovered that? Still, not a bit the less will they presently be laying the child[63] here before the door. Of this, then, I now warn you, master, that it will happen, that you may be aware of it. Don't you hereafter be saying that this was done through the advice or artifices of Davus. I wish this suspicion of yours to be entirely removed from myself.

SIMO

How do you know that?

DAVUS

I've heard so, and I believe it: many things combine for me to form this conjecture. In the first place then, she declared that she was pregnant by Pamphilus; that has been proved to be false.[64] Now, when she sees that preparations are being made for the wedding at our house, the maid-servant is directly sent to fetch the midwife to her, and to bring a child at the same time.[65] Unless it is managed for you to see the child, the marriage will not be at all impeded.

SIMO

What do you say to this? When you perceived that they were adopting this plan, why didn't you tell Pamphilus immediately?

DAVUS

Why, who has induced him to leave her, but myself? For, indeed, we all know how desperately he loved her. Now he wishes for a wife. In fine, do you intrust me with that affair; proceed however, as before, to celebrate these nuptials, just as you are doing, and I trust that the Gods will prosper this matter.

SIMO

Very well; be off in-doors; wait for me there, and get ready what's necessary to be prepared.

[**DAVUS** goes into the house.

He hasn't prevailed upon me even now altogether to believe these things, and I don't know whether what he has said is all true; but I deem it of little moment; this is of far greater importance to me—that my son himself has promised me. Now I'll go and find Chremes; I'll ask him for a wife for my son; if I obtain my request, at what other time rather than to-day should I prefer these nuptials taking place? For as my son has promised, I have no doubt but that if he should prove unwilling, I can fairly compel him. And look! here's Chremes himself, just at the very time.

SCENE V

Enter **CHREMES**.

SIMO

I greet you, Chremes.

CHREMES

O, you are the very person I was looking for.

SIMO
And I for you.

CHREMES
You meet me at a welcome moment. Some persons have been to me, to say that they had heard from you, that my daughter was to be married to your son to-day; I've come to see whether they are out of their senses or you.

SIMO
Listen; in a few words you shall learn both what I want of you, and what you seek to know.

CHREMES
I am listening; say what you wish.

SIMO
By the Gods, I do entreat you, Chremes, and by our friendship, which, commencing with our infancy, has grown up with our years, and by your only daughter and by my own son (of preserving whom the entire power lies with you), that you will assist me in this matter; and that, just as this marriage was about to be celebrated, it may be celebrated.

CHREMES
O, don't importune me; as though you needed to obtain this of me by entreaty. Do you suppose I am different now from what I was formerly, when I promised her? If it is for the advantage of them both that it should take place, order her to be sent for. But if from this course there would result more harm than advantage for each, this I do beg of you, that you will consult for their common good, as though she were your own daughter, and I the father of Pamphilus.

SIMO
Nay, so I intend, and so I wish it to be, Chremes; and I would not ask it of you, did not the occasion itself require it.

CHREMES
What is the matter?

SIMO
There is a quarrel between Glycerium and my son.

CHREMES [Ironically]
I hear you.

SIMO
So much so, that I'm in hopes they may be separated.

CHREMES
Nonsense!

SIMO

It really is so.

CHREMES
After this fashion, i'faith, I tell you, "the quarrels of lovers are the renewal of love."

SIMO
Well—this I beg of you, that we may prevent it. While an opportunity offers, and while his passion is cooled by affronts, before the wiles of these women and their tears, craftily feigned, bring back his love-sick mind to compassion, let us give him a wife. I trust, Chremes, that, when attached by intimacy and a respectable marriage, he will easily extricate himself from these evils.

CHREMES
So it appears to you; but I do not think[66] that either he can possibly hold to her with constancy, or that I can put up with it if he does not.

SIMO
How then can you be sure of that, unless you make the experiment?

CHREMES
But for that experiment to be made upon a daughter is a serious thing—

SIMO
Why look, all the inconvenience in fine amounts to this—possibly, which may the Gods forfend, a separation may take place. But if he is reformed, see how many are the advantages: in the first place, you will have restored a son to your friend; you will obtain a sure son-in-law[67] for yourself, and a husband for your daughter.

CHREMES
What is one to say to all this? If you feel persuaded that this is beneficial, I don't wish that any advantage should be denied you.

SIMO
With good reason, Chremes, have I always considered you a most valuable friend.

CHREMES
But how say you—?

SIMO
What?

CHREMES
How do you know that they are now at variance?

SIMO
Davus himself, who is privy to all their plans, has told me so; and he advises me to expedite the match as fast as I can. Do you think he would do so, unless he was aware that my son desired it? You yourself as well shall presently hear what he says.

[Goes to the door of his house and calls.

Halloo there! Call Davus out here. Look, here he is; I see him just coming out.

SCENE VI

Enter **DAVUS** from the house.

DAVUS
I was coming to you.

SIMO
Why, what's the matter?

DAVUS
Why isn't the bride sent for?[68] It's now growing late in the day.

SIMO
Do you hear me? I've been for some time not a little apprehensive of you, Davus, lest you should do that which the common class of servants is in the habit of doing, namely, impose upon me by your artifices; because my son is engaged in an amour.

DAVUS
What, I do that?

SIMO
I fancied so; and therefore, fearing that, I concealed from you what I shall now mention.

DAVUS
What?

SIMO
You shall know; for now I almost feel confidence in you.

DAVUS
Have you found out at last what sort of a person I am?

SIMO
The marriage was not to have taken place.

DAVUS
How? Not to have taken place?

SIMO
But I was making pretense, that I might test you all.

DAVUS [Affecting surprise]
What is it you tell me?

SIMO
Such is the fact.

DAVUS
Only see! I was not able to discover that. Dear me! what a cunning contrivance!

SIMO
Listen to this. Just as I ordered you to go from here into the house, he—
[Pointing to **CHREMES**]
—most opportunely met me.

DAVUS [Aside]
Ha! Are we undone, then?

SIMO
I told him what you just now told me.

DAVUS [Aside]
Why, what am I to hear?

SIMO
I begged him to give his daughter, and with difficulty I prevailed upon him.

DAVUS [Aside]
Utterly ruined!

SIMO [Overhearing him speaking]
Eh—What was it you said?

DAVUS
Extremely well done, I say.

SIMO
There's no delay on his part now.

CHREMES
I'll go home at once; I'll tell her to make due preparation, and bring back word here.

[Exit.

SIMO
Now I do entreat you, Davus, since you by yourself have brought about this marriage for me—

DAVUS
I myself, indeed![69]

SIMO

Do your best still to reform my son.

DAVUS

Troth, I'll do it with all due care.

SIMO

Do it now, while his mind is agitated.

DAVUS

You may be at ease.

SIMO

Come then; where is he just now?

DAVUS

A wonder if he isn't at home.

SIMO

I'll go to him; and what I've been telling you, I'll tell him as well.

[Goes into his house.

DAVUS alone.

DAVUS [To himself]

I'm a lost man! What reason is there why I shouldn't take my departure straightway hence for the mill? There's no room left for supplicating; I've upset every thing now; I've deceived my master; I've plunged my master's son into a marriage; I've been the cause of its taking place this very day, without his hoping for it, and against the wish of Pamphilus. Here's cleverness for you! But, if I had kept myself quiet, no mischief would have happened.
[Starting]
But see, I espy him; I'm utterly undone! Would that there were some spot here for me, from which I might this instant pitch myself headlong!

[Stands apart.

Enter **PAMPHILUS** in haste from **SIMO'S** house.

PAMPHILUS
Where is he? The villain, who this day—I'm ruined; and I confess that this has justly befallen me, for being such a dolt, so devoid of sense; that I should have intrusted my fortunes to a frivolous slave![70] I am suffering the reward of my folly; still he shall never get off from me unpunished for this.

DAVUS [Apart]
I'm quite sure that I shall be safe in future, if for the present I get clear of this mishap.

PAMPHILUS
But what now am I to say to my father? Am I to deny that I am ready, who have just promised to marry? With what effrontery could I presume to do that? I know not what to do with myself.

DAVUS [Apart]
Nor I with myself, and yet I'm giving all due attention to it. I'll tell him that I will devise something, in order that I may procure some respite in this dilemma.

PAMPHILUS [Catching sight of him]
Oho!

DAVUS [Apart]
I'm seen.

PAMPHILUS [Sneeringly]
How now, good sir, what are you about? Do you see how dreadfully I am hampered by your devices?

DAVUS
Still, I'll soon extricate you.

PAMPHILUS
You, extricate me?

DAVUS
Assuredly, Pamphilus.

PAMPHILUS
As you have just done, I suppose.

DAVUS
Why no, better, I trust.

PAMPHILUS
What, am I to believe you, you scoundrel?[71] You, indeed, make good a matter that's all embarrassment and ruin! Just see, in whom I've been placing reliance—you who this day from a most happy state have been and plunged me into a marriage. Didn't I say that this would be the case?

DAVUS
You did say so.

PAMPHILUS
What do you deserve?[72]

DAVUS
The cross.[73] But allow me a little time to recover myself; I'll soon hit upon something.

PAMPHILUS
Ah me! not to have the leisure to inflict punishment upon you as I desire! for the present conjuncture warns me to take precautions for myself, not to be taking vengeance on you.

[Exeunt.

ACT THE FOURTH

SCENE I

Enter **CHARINUS**, wringing his hands.

CHARINUS [To himself]
Is this to be believed or spoken of; that malice so great could be inborn in any one as to exult at misfortunes, and to derive advantage from the distresses of another! Oh, is this true? Assuredly, that is the most dangerous class of men, in whom there is only a slight degree of hesitation at refusing; afterward, when the time arrives for fulfilling their promises, then, obliged, of necessity they discover themselves. They are afraid, and yet the circumstances[74] compel them to refuse. Then, in that case, their very insolent remark is, "Who are you? What are you to me? What should I give up to you what's my own? Look you, I am the most concerned in my own interests."[75] But if you inquire where is honor, they are not ashamed.[76] Here, where there is occasion, they are not afraid; there, where there is no occasion, they are afraid. But what am I to do? Ought I not to go to him, and reason with him upon this outrage, and heap many an invective upon him? Yet some one may say, "you will avail nothing." Nothing? At least I shall have vexed him, and have given vent to my own feelings.

SCENE II

Enter **PAMPHILUS** and **DAVUS**.

PAMPHILUS
Charinus, unintentionally I have ruined both myself and you, unless the Gods in some way befriend us.

CHARINUS
Unintentionally, is it! An excuse has been discovered at last. You have broken your word.

PAMPHILUS
How so, pray?

CHARINUS

Do you expect to deceive me a second time by these speeches?

PAMPHILUS

What does this mean?

CHARINUS

Since I told you that I loved her, she has become quite pleasing to you. Ah wretched me! to have judged of your disposition from my own.

PAMPHILUS

You are mistaken.

CHARINUS

Did this pleasure appear to you not to be quite complete, unless you tantalized me in my passion, and lured me on by groundless hopes?—You may take her.

PAMPHILUS

I, take her? Alas! you know not in what perplexities, to my sorrow, I am involved, and what vast anxieties this executioner of mine—
[Pointing to **DAVUS**]
—has contrived for me by his devices.

CHARINUS

What is it so wonderful, if he takes example from yourself?

PAMPHILUS

You would not say that if you understood either myself or my affection.

CHARINUS

I'm quite aware
[Ironically];
You have just now had a dispute with your father, and he is now angry with you in consequence, and has not been able to-day to prevail upon you to marry her.

PAMPHILUS

No, not at all,—as you are not acquainted with my sorrows, these nuptials were not in preparation for me; and no one was thinking at present of giving me a wife.

CHARINUS

I am aware; you have been influenced by your own inclination.

PAMPHILUS

Hold; you do not yet know all.

CHARINUS

For my part, I certainly do know that you are about to marry her.

PAMPHILUS
Why are you torturing me to death? Listen to this. He—
[Pointing to **DAVUS**]
—never ceased to urge me to tell my father that I would marry her; to advise and persuade me, even until he compelled me.

CHARINUS
Who was this person?

PAMPHILUS
Davus.

CHARINUS
Davus! For what reason?

PAMPHILUS
I don't know; except that I must have been under the displeasure of the Gods, for me to have listened to him.

CHARINUS
Is this the fact, Davus?

DAVUS
It is the fact.

CHARINUS [Starting]
Ha! What do you say, you villain? Then may the Gods send you an end worthy of your deeds. Come now, tell me, if all his enemies had wished him to be plunged into a marriage, what advice but this could they have given?

DAVUS
I have been deceived, but I don't despair.

CHARINUS [Ironically]
I'm sure of that.

DAVUS
This way it has not succeeded; we'll try another. Unless, perhaps, you think that because it failed at first, this misfortune can not now possibly be changed for better luck.

PAMPHILUS
Certainly not; for I quite believe that if you set about it, you will be making two marriages for me out of one.

DAVUS
I owe you this, Pamphilus, in respect of my servitude, to strive with hands and feet, night and day; to submit to hazard of my life, to serve you. It is your part, if any thing has fallen out contrary to

expectation, to forgive me. What I was contriving has not succeeded; still, I am using all endeavors; or, do you yourself devise something better, and dismiss me.

PAMPHILUS
I wish to; restore me to the position in which you found me.

DAVUS
I'll do so.

PAMPHILUS
But it must be done directly.

DAVUS
But the door of Glycerium's house here makes a noise.[77]

PAMPHILUS
That's nothing to you.

DAVUS [Assuming an attitude of meditation]
I'm in search of—

PAMPHILUS [Ironically]
Dear me, what, now at last?

DAVUS
Presently I'll give you what I've hit upon.

SCENE III

Enter **MYSIS** from the house of **GLYCERIUM**.

MYSIS [Calling at the door to **GLYCERIUM** within]
Now, wherever he is, I'll take care that your own Pamphilus shall be found for you, and brought to you by me; do you only, my life, cease to vex yourself.

PAMPHILUS
Mysis.

MYSIS [Turning round]
Who is it? Why, Pamphilus, you do present yourself opportunely to me. My mistress charged me to beg of you, if you love her, to come to her directly; she says she wishes to see you.

PAMPHILUS [Aside]
Alas! I am undone; this dilemma grows apace!
[To **DAVUS**]

For me and her, unfortunate persons, now to be tortured this way through your means; for I am sent for, because she has discovered that my marriage is in preparation.

CHARINUS
From which, indeed, how easily a respite could have been obtained, if he—
[Pointing to **DAVUS**]
—had kept himself quiet.

DAVUS [Ironically to **CHARINUS**]
Do proceed; if he isn't sufficiently angry of his own accord, do you irritate him.

MYSIS [To **PAMPHILUS**]
Aye faith, that is the case; and for that reason, poor thing, she is now in distress.

PAMPHILUS
Mysis, I swear by all the Gods that I will never forsake her; not if I were to know that all men would be my enemies in consequence. Her have I chosen for mine; she has fallen to my lot; our feelings are congenial; farewell they, who wish for a separation between us; nothing but Death separates her from me.

MYSIS
I begin to revive.

PAMPHILUS
Not the responses of Apollo are more true than this. If it can possibly be contrived that my father may not believe that this marriage has been broken off through me, I could wish it. But if that can not be, I will do that which is easily effected, for him to believe that through me it has been caused. What do you think of me?

CHARINUS
That you are as unhappy as myself.

DAVUS [Placing his finger on his forehead]
I'm contriving an expedient.

CHARINUS
You are a clever hand; if you do set about any thing.

DAVUS
Assuredly, I'll manage this for you.

PAMPHILUS
There's need of it now.

DAVUS
But I've got it now.

CHARINUS

What is it?

DAVUS
For him—
[Pointing to **PAMPHILUS**]
I've got it, not for you, don't mistake.

CHARINUS
I'm quite satisfied.

PAMPHILUS
What will you do? Tell me.

DAVUS
I'm afraid that this day won't be long enough for me to execute it, so don't suppose that I've now got leisure for relating it; do you betake yourself off at once, for you are a hinderance to me.

PAMPHILUS
I'll go and see her.

[Goes into the house of **GLYCERIUM**.

DAVUS [To **CHARINUS**]
What are you going to do? Whither are you going from here?

CHARINUS
Do you wish me to tell you the truth?

DAVUS
No, not at all;—
[Aside]
—he's making the beginning of a long story for me.

CHARINUS
What will become of me?

DAVUS
Come now, you unreasonable person, are you not satisfied that I give you a little respite, by putting off his marriage?

CHARINUS
But yet, Davus—

DAVUS
What then?

CHARINUS
That I may marry her—

DAVUS
Absurd.

CHARINUS
Be sure to come hither—
[Pointing in the direction of his house]
—to my house, if you can effect any thing.

DAVUS
Why should I come? I can do nothing for you.

CHARINUS
But still, if any thing—

DAVUS
Well, well, I'll come.

CHARINUS
If you can; I shall be at home.

[Exit.

SCENE IV

MYSIS and **DAVUS**.

DAVUS
Do you, Mysis, remain here a little while, until I come out.

MYSIS
For what reason?

DAVUS
There's a necessity for so doing.

MYSIS
Make haste.

DAVUS
I'll be here this moment, I tell you.

[He goes into the house of **GLYCERIUM**.

MYSIS alone.

MYSIS [To herself]
That nothing can be secure to any one! Ye Gods, by our trust in you! I used to make sure that this Pamphilus was a supreme blessing for my mistress; a friend, a protector, a husband secured under every circumstance; yet what anguish is she, poor thing, now suffering through him? Clearly there's more trouble for her now than there was happiness formerly. But Davus is coming out.

SCENE VI

Enter **DAVUS** from the house of **GLYCERIUM** with the child.

MYSIS
My good sir, prithee, what is that? Whither are you carrying the child?

DAVUS
Mysis, I now stand in need of your cunning being brought into play in this matter, and of your address.

MYSIS
Why, what are you going to do?

DAVUS [Holding out the child]
Take it from me directly, and lay it down before our door.

MYSIS
Prithee, on the ground?

DAVUS [Pointing]
Take some sacred herbs[78] from the altar here,[79] and strew them under it.

MYSIS
Why don't you do it yourself?

DAVUS
That if perchance I should have to swear to my master that I did not place it there, I may be enabled to do so with a clear conscience.

MYSIS
I understand; have these new scruples only just now occurred to you, pray?

DAVUS
Bestir yourself quickly, that you may learn what I'm going to do next.
[**MYSIS** lays the child at **SIMO'S** door]
Oh Jupiter!

MYSIS [Starting up]
What's the matter?

DAVUS
The father of the intended bride is coming in the middle of it all. The plan which I had first purposed I now give up.[80]

MYSIS
I don't understand what you are talking about.

DAVUS
I'll pretend too that I've come in this direction from the right. Do you take care to help out the conversation by your words, whenever there's necessity.[81]

MYSIS
I don't at all comprehend what you are about; but if there's any thing in which you have need of my assistance, as you understand the best, I'll stay, that I mayn't in any way impede your success.

[**DAVUS** retires out of sight.

SCENE VII

Enter **CHREMES** on the other side of the stage, going toward the house of **SIMO**.

CHREMES [To himself]
After having provided the things necessary for my daughter's nuptials, I'm returning, that I may request her to be sent for.
[Seeing the **CHILD**]
But what's this? I'faith, it's a child.
[Addressing **MYSIS**]
Woman, have you laid that here—
[Pointing to the **CHILD**]?

MYSIS [Aside, looking out for **DAVUS**]
Where is he?

CHREMES
Don't you answer me?

MYSIS [Looking about, to herself]
He isn't any where to be seen. Woe to wretched me! the fellow has left me and is off.

DAVUS [Coming forward and pretending not to see them]
Ye Gods, by our trust in you! what a crowd there is in the Forum! What a lot of people are squabbling there!

[Aloud]
Then provisions are so dear.
[Aside]
What to say besides, I don't know.

[CHREMES passes by MYSIS, and goes to a distance at the back of the stage.

MYSIS
Pray, why did you leave me here alone?

DAVUS [Pretending to start on seeing the child]
Ha! what story is this? How now, Mysis, whence comes this child? Who has brought it here?

MYSIS
Are you quite right in your senses, to be asking me that?

DAVUS
Whom, then, ought I to ask, as I don't see any one else here?

CHREMES [Apart to himself]
I wonder whence it has come.

DAVUS
Are you going to tell me what I ask?

MYSIS
Pshaw!

DAVUS [In a whisper]
Step aside to the right.

[They retire on one side.

MYSIS
You are out of your senses; didn't you your own self?

DAVUS [In a low voice]
Take you care not to utter a single word beyond what I ask you. Why don't you say aloud whence it comes?

MYSIS [In a loud voice]
From our house.

DAVUS [Affecting indignation]
Heyday, indeed! it really is a wonder if a woman, who is a courtesan, acts impudently.

CHREMES
So far as I can learn, this woman belongs to the Andrian.

DAVUS
Do we seem to you such very suitable persons for you to be playing tricks with us in this way?

CHREMES [Apart]
I came just in time.

DAVUS
Make haste then, and take the child away from the door here:—
[In a low voice]
—stay there; take care you don't stir from that spot.

MYSIS [Aside]
May the Gods confound you! you do so terrify poor me.

DAVUS [In a loud voice]
Is it to you I speak or not?

MYSIS
What is it you want?

DAVUS [Aloud]
What—do you ask me again? Tell me, whose child have you been laying here? Let me know.

MYSIS
Don't you know?

DAVUS [In a low voice]
Have done with what I know; tell me what I ask.

MYSIS [Aloud]
It belongs to your people.

DAVUS [Aloud]
Which of our people?

MYSIS [Aloud]
To Pamphilus.

DAVUS [Affecting surprise in a loud tone]
How? What—to Pamphilus?

MYSIS [Aloud]
How now—is it not so?

CHREMES [Apart]
With good reason have I always been averse to this match, it's clear.

DAVUS [Calling aloud]
O abominable piece of effrontery!

MYSIS
Why are you bawling out so?

DAVUS [Aloud]
What, the very one I saw being carried to your house yesterday evening?

MYSIS
O you impudent fellow!

DAVUS [Aloud]
It's the truth. I saw Canthara stuffed out beneath her clothes.[82]

MYSIS
I'faith, I thank the Gods that several free women were present[83] at the delivery.

DAVUS [Aloud]
Assuredly she doesn't know him, on whose account she resorts to these schemes. Chremes, she fancies, if he sees the child laid before the door, will not give his daughter; i'faith, he'll give her all the sooner.

CHREMES [Apart]
I'faith, he'll not do so.

DAVUS [Aloud]
Now therefore, that you may be quite aware, if you don't take up the child, I'll roll it forthwith into the middle of the road; and yourself in the same place I'll roll over into the mud.

MYSIS
Upon my word, man, you are not sober.

DAVUS [Aloud]
One scheme brings on another. I now hear it whispered about that she is a citizen of Attica—

CHREMES [Apart]
Ha!

DAVUS [Aloud]
And that, constrained by the laws,[84] he will have to take her as his wife.

MYSIS
Well now, pray, is she not a citizen?

CHREMES [Apart]
I had almost fallen unawares into a comical misfortune.

[Comes forward.

DAVUS
Who's that, speaking?
[Pretending to look about]
O Chremes, you have come in good time. Do listen to this.

CHREMES
I have heard it all already.

DAVUS
Prithee, did you hear it? Here's villainy for you! she—
[Pointing at **MYSIS**]
—ought to be carried off[85] hence to the torture forthwith.
[To **MYSIS**, pointing at **CHREMES**]
This is Chremes himself; don't suppose that you are trifling with Davus only.

MYSIS
Wretched me! upon my faith I have told no untruth, my worthy old gentleman.

CHREMES
I know the whole affair. Is Simo within?

DAVUS
He is.

[**CHREMES** goes into **SIMO'S** house.

SCENE VIII

DAVUS and **MYSIS**.

MYSIS [**DAVUS** attempting to caress her]
Don't touch me, villain.

[Moving away.

On my word, if I don't tell Glycerium all this....

DAVUS
How now, simpleton, don't you know what has been done?

MYSIS
How should I know?

DAVUS

This is the bride's father. It couldn't any other way have been managed that he should know the things that we wanted him to know.

MYSIS
You should have told me that before.

DAVUS
Do you suppose that it makes little difference whether you do things according to impulse, as nature prompts, or from premeditation?

SCENE IX

Enter **CRITO**, looking about him.

CRITO [To himself]
It was said that Chrysis used to live in this street, who preferred to gain wealth here dishonorably to living honestly as a poor woman in her own country: by her death that property has descended to me by law.[86] But I see some persons of whom to make inquiry.
[Accosting them]
Good-morrow to you.

MYSIS
Prithee, whom do I see? Isn't this Crito, the kinsman of Chrysis? It is he.

CRITO
O Mysis, greetings to you.

MYSIS
Welcome to you, Crito.

CRITO
Is Chrysis then—?[87] Alas!

MYSIS
Too truly. She has indeed left us poor creatures quite heart-broken.

CRITO
How fare you here, and in what fashion? Pretty well?

MYSIS
What, we? Just as we can, as they say; since we can't as we would.

CRITO
How is Glycerium? Has she discovered her parents yet?

MYSIS

I wish she had.

CRITO
What, not yet? With no favorable omen did I set out for this place; for, upon my faith, if I had known that, I never would have moved a foot hither. She was always said to be, and was looked upon as her sister; what things were hers she is in possession of; now for me to begin a suit at law here, the precedents of others warn me, a stranger,[88] how easy and profitable a task it would be for me. At the same time, I suppose that by this she has got some friend and protector; for she was pretty nearly a grown-up girl when she left there. They would cry out that I am a sharper; that, a pauper, I'm hunting after an inheritance; besides, I shouldn't like to strip the girl herself.

MYSIS
O most worthy stranger! I'faith, Crito, you still adhere to your good old-fashioned ways.

CRITO
Lead me to her, since I have come hither, that I may see her.

MYSIS
By all means.

[They go into the house of **GLYCERIUM**.

DAVUS [To himself]
I'll follow them; I don't wish the old man to see me at this moment.

[He follows **MYSIS** and **CRITO**.

ACT THE FIFTH

SCENE I

Enter **CHREMES** and **SIMO** from the house of **SIMO**.

CHREMES
Enough already, enough, Simo, has my friendship toward you been proved. Sufficient hazard have I begun to encounter; make an end of your entreaties, then. While I've been endeavoring to oblige you, I've almost fooled away my daughter's prospects in life.

SIMO
Nay but, now in especial, Chremes, I do beg and entreat of you, that the favor, commenced a short time since in words, you'll now complete by deeds.

CHREMES
See how unreasonable you are from your very earnestness; so long as you effect what you desire, you neither think of limits to compliance, nor what it is you request of me; for if you did think, you would now forbear to trouble me with unreasonable requests.

SIMO
What unreasonable requests?

CHREMES
Do you ask? You importuned me to promise my daughter to a young man engaged in another attachment, averse to the marriage state, to plunge her into discord and a marriage of uncertain duration; that through her sorrow and her anguish I might reclaim your son. You prevailed; while the case admitted of it I made preparations. Now it does not admit of it; you must put up with it; they say that she is a citizen of this place; a child has been born; do cease to trouble us.

SIMO
By the Gods, I do conjure you not to bring your mind to believe those whose especial interest it is that he should be as degraded as possible. On account of the marriage, have all these things been feigned and contrived. When the reason for which they do these things is removed from them, they will desist.

CHREMES
You are mistaken: I myself saw the servant-maid wrangling with Davus.

SIMO [Sneeringly]
I am aware.

CHREMES
With an appearance of earnestness, when neither at the moment perceived that I was present there.

SIMO
I believe it; and Davus a short time since forewarned me that this would be the case; and I don't know how I forgot to tell it you to-day, as I had intended.

SCENE II

Enter **DAVUS** from the house of **GLYCERIUM**.

DAVUS [Aloud at the door, not seeing **SIMO** and **CHREMES**]
Now then, I bid you set your minds at ease.

CHREMES [To **SIMO**]
See you, there's Davus.

SIMO
From what house is he coming out?

DAVUS [To himself]
Through my means, and that of the stranger—

SIMO [Overhearing]

What mischief is this?

DAVUS [To himself]
I never did see a more opportune person, encounter, or occasion.

SIMO
The rascal! I wonder who it is he's praising?

DAVUS
All the affair is now in a safe position.

SIMO
Why do I delay to accost him?

DAVUS [To himself, catching sight of **SIMO**]
It's my master; What am I to do?

SIMO [Accosting him]
O, save you, good sir!

DAVUS [Affecting surprise]
Hah! Simo! O, Chremes, my dear sir, all things are now quite ready in-doors.

SIMO [Ironically]
You have taken such very good care.

DAVUS
Send for the bride when you like.

SIMO
Very good:
[Ironically]
—of course, that's the only thing that's now wanting here. But do you answer me this, what business had you there?

[Pointing to the house of **GLYCERIUM**.

DAVUS
What, I?

SIMO
Just so.

DAVUS
I?

SIMO
Yes, you.

DAVUS
I went in just now.

SIMO
As if I asked how long ago!

DAVUS
Together with your son.

SIMO
What, is Phamphilus in there?
[Aside]
To my confusion, I'm on the rack
[To **DAVUS**]
How now? Didn't you say that there was enmity between them, you scoundrel?

DAVUS
There is.

SIMO
Why is he there, then?

CHREMES
Why do you suppose he is?
[Ironically]
Quarreling with her, of course.

DAVUS
Nay but, Chremes, I'll let you now hear from me a disgraceful piece of business. An old man, I don't know who he is, has just now come here; look you, he is a confident and shrewd person; when you look at his appearance, he seems to be a person of some consequence. There is a grave sternness in his features, and something commanding in his words.

SIMO
What news are you bringing, I wonder?

DAVUS
Why nothing but what I heard him mention.

SIMO
What does he say then?

DAVUS
That he knows Glycerium to be a citizen of Attica.

SIMO [Going to his door]
Ho there! Dromo, Dromo!

Enter **DROMO** hastily from the house.

DROMO
What is it?

SIMO
Dromo!

DAVUS
Hear me.

SIMO
If you add a word—Dromo!

DAVUS
Hear me, pray.

DROMO [To **SIMO**]
What do you want?

SIMO [Pointing to **DAVUS**]
Carry him off on your shoulders in-doors as fast as possible.

DROMO
Whom?

SIMO
Davus.

DAVUS
For what reason?

SIMO
Because I choose.
[To **DROMO**]
Carry him off, I say.

DAVUS
What have I done?

SIMO
Carry him off.

DAVUS
If you find that I have told a lie in any one matter, then kill me.

SIMO
I'll hear nothing. I'll soon have you set in motion.[89]

DAVUS
What? Although this is the truth.

SIMO
In spite of it.
[To **DROMO**]
Take care he's kept well secured; and, do you hear? Tie him up hands and feet together.[90] Now then, be off; upon my faith this very day, if I live, I'll teach you what hazard there is in deceiving a master, and him in deceiving a father.

[**DROMO** leads **DAVUS** into the house.

CHREMES
Oh, don't be so extremely vexed.

SIMO
O Chremes, the dutifulness of a son! Do you not pity me? That I should endure so much trouble for such a son!

[Goes to the door of **GLYCERIUM'S** house.

Come, Pamphilus, come out, Pamphilus! have you any shame left?

SCENE IV

Enter **PAMPHILUS** in haste from **GLYCERIUM'S** house.

PAMPHILUS
Who is it that wants me?
[Aside]
I'm undone! it's my father.

SIMO
What say you, of all men, the—?

CHREMES
Oh! rather speak about the matter itself, and forbear to use harsh language.

SIMO

As if any thing too severe could now be possibly said against him. Pray, do you say that Glycerium is a citizen—

PAMPHILUS
So they say.

SIMO
So they say! Unparalleled assurance! does he consider what he says? Is he sorry for what he has done? Does his countenance, pray, at all betray any marks of shame? That he should be of mind so weak, as, without regard to the custom and the law[91] of his fellow-citizens, and the wish of his own father, to be anxious, in spite of every thing, to have her, to his own utter disgrace!

PAMPHILUS
Miserable that I am!

SIMO
Ha! have you at last found that out only just now, Pamphilus? Long since did that expression, long since, when you made up your mind, that what you desired must be effected by you at any price; from that very day did that expression aptly befit you. But yet why do I torment myself? Why vex myself? Why worry my old age with this madness? Am I to suffer the punishment for his offenses? Nay then, let him have her, good-by to him, let him pass his life with her.

PAMPHILUS
My father—

SIMO
How, "my father?" As if you stood in any need of this father. Home, wife, and children, provided by you against the will of your father! People suborned, too, to say that she is a citizen of this place! You have gained your point.

PAMPHILUS
Father, may I say a few words?

SIMO
What can you say to me?

CHREMES
But, Simo, do hear him.

SIMO
I, hear him? Why should I hear him, Chremes?

CHREMES
Still, however, do allow him to speak.

SIMO
Well then, let him speak: I allow him.

PAMPHILUS

I own that I love her; if that is committing a fault, I own that also. To you, father, do I subject myself. Impose on me any injunction you please; command me. Do you wish me to take a wife? Do you wish me to give her up? As well as I can, I will endure it. This only I request of you, not to think that this old gentleman has been suborned by me. Allow me to clear myself, and to bring him here before you.

SIMO

To bring him here?

PAMPHILUS

Do allow me, father.

CHREMES

He asks what's reasonable; do give him leave.

PAMPHILUS

Allow me to obtain thus much of you.

SIMO

I allow it. I desire any thing, so long as I find, Chremes, that I have not been deceived by him.

[**PAMPHILUS** goes into the house of **GLYCERIUM**.

CHREMES

For a great offense, a slight punishment ought to satisfy a father.

SCENE V

Re-enter **PAMPHILUS** with **CRITO**.

CRITO [To **PAMPHILUS**, as he is coming out]
Forbear entreating. Of these, any one reason prompts me to do it, either your own sake, or the fact that it is the truth, or that I wish well for Glycerium herself.

CHREMES [Starting]
Do I see Crito of Andros? Surely it is he.

CRITO
Greetings to you, Chremes.

CHREMES
How is it that, so contrary to your usage, you are at Athens?

CRITO
So it has happened. But is this Simo?

CHREMES
It is he.

CRITO
Simo, were you asking for me?

SIMO
How now, do you say that Glycerium is a citizen of this place?

CRITO
Do you deny it?

SIMO [Ironically]
Have you come here so well prepared?

CRITO
For what purpose?

SIMO
Do you ask? Are you to be acting this way with impunity? Are you to be luring young men into snares here, inexperienced in affairs, and liberally brought up, by tempting them, and to be playing upon their fancies by making promises?

CRITO
Are you in your senses?

SIMO
And are you to be patching up amours with Courtesans by marriage?

PAMPHILUS [Aside]
I'm undone! I fear that the stranger will not put up with this.

CHREMES
If, Simo, you knew this person well, you would not think thus; he is a worthy man.

SIMO
He, a worthy man! To come so opportunely to-day just at the very nuptials, and yet never to have come before?
[Ironically]
Of course, we must believe him, Chremes.

PAMPHILUS [Aside]
If I didn't dread my father, I have something, which, in this conjuncture, I could opportunely suggest to him.[92]

SIMO [Sneeringly, to **CHREMES**]
A sharper![93]

CRITO [Starting]
Hah!

CHREMES
It is his way, Crito; do excuse it.

CRITO
Let him take heed how he behaves. If he persists in saying to me what he likes, he'll be hearing things that he don't like. Am I meddling with these matters or interesting myself? Can you not endure your troubles with a patient mind? For as to what I say, whether it is true or false what I have heard, can soon be known. A certain man of Attica, a long time ago,[94] his ship being wrecked, was cast ashore at Andros, and this woman together with him, who was then a little girl; he, in his destitution, by chance first made application to the father of Chrysis—

SIMO [Ironically]
He's beginning his tale.

CHREMES
Let him alone.

CRITO
Really, is he to be interrupting me in this way?

CHREMES
Do you proceed.

CRITO
He who received him was a relation of mine. There I heard from him that he was a native of Attica. He died there.

CHREMES
His name?

CRITO
The name, in such a hurry!

PAMPHILUS
Phania.

CHREMES [Starting]
Hah! I shall die!

CRITO
I'faith, I really think it was Phania; this I know for certain, he said that he was a citizen of Rhamnus.[95]

CHREMES
O Jupiter!

CRITO
Many other persons in Andros have heard the same, Chremes.

CHREMES [Aside]
I trust it may turn out as I hope.
[To **CRITO**]
Come now, tell me, what did he then say about her? Did he say she was his own daughter?

CRITO
No.

CHREMES
Whose then?

CRITO
His brother's daughter.

CHREMES
She certainly is mine.

CRITO
What do you say?

SIMO
What is this that you say?

PAMPHILUS [Aside]
Prick up your ears, Pamphilus.

SIMO
Why do you suppose so?

CHREMES
That Phania was my brother.

SIMO
I knew him, and I am aware of it.

CHREMES
He, flying from the wars, and following me to Asia, set out from here. At the same time he was afraid to leave her here behind; since then, this is the first time I have heard what became of him.

PAMPHILUS [Aside]
I am scarcely myself, so much has my mind been agitated by fear, hope, joy, and surprise at this so great, so unexpected blessing.

SIMO
Really, I am glad for many reasons that she has been discovered to be a citizen.

PAMPHILUS
I believe it, father.

CHREMES
But there yet remains one difficulty[96] with me, which keeps me in suspense.

PAMPHILUS [Aside]
You deserve to be —, with your scruples, you plague. You are seeking a knot in a bulrush.[97]

CRITO [To **CHREMES**]
What is that?

CHREMES
The names don't agree.

CRITO
Troth, she had another when little.

CHREMES
What was it, Crito? Can you remember it?

CRITO
I'm trying to recollect it.

PAMPHILUS [Aside]
Am I to suffer his memory to stand in the way of my happiness, when I myself can provide my own remedy in this matter? I will not suffer it.
[Aloud]
Hark you, Chremes, that which you are trying to recollect is "Pasibula."

CHREMES
The very same.

CRITO
That's it.

PAMPHILUS
I've heard it from herself a thousand times.

SIMO
I suppose, Chremes, that you believe that we all rejoice at this discovery.

CHREMES
So may the Gods bless me, I do believe it.

PAMPHILUS
What remains to be done, father?

SIMO
The event itself has quite brought me to reconcilement.

PAMPHILUS
O kind father! With regard to her as a wife, since I have taken possession of her, Chremes will not offer any opposition.

CHREMES
The plea is a very good one, unless perchance your father says any thing to the contrary.

PAMPHILUS
Of course, I agree.

SIMO
Then be it so.[98]

CHREMES
Her portion, Pamphilus, is ten talents.

PAMPHILUS
I am satisfied.

CHREMES
I'll hasten to my daughter. Come now,—
[Beckoning]
—along with me, Crito; for I suppose that she will not know me.

[They go into **GLYCERIUM'S** house.

SIMO [To **PAMPHILUS**]
Why don't you order her to be sent for hither, to our house?

PAMPHILUS
Well thought of; I'll at once give charge of that to Davus.

SIMO
He can't do it.

PAMPHILUS
How so?

SIMO
Because he has another matter that more nearly concerns himself, and of more importance.

PAMPHILUS
What, pray?

SIMO
He is bound.

PAMPHILUS
Father, he is not rightly bound.[99]

SIMO
But I ordered to that effect.

PAMPHILUS
Prithee, do order him to be set at liberty.

SIMO
Well, be it so.

PAMPHILUS
But immediately.

SIMO
I'm going in.

PAMPHILUS
O fortunate and happy day!

[**SIMO** goes into his house.

SCENE VI

Enter **CHARINUS**, at a distance.

CHARINUS [Apart to himself]
I'm come to see what Pamphilus is about; and look, here he is.

PAMPHILUS [To himself]
Some one perhaps might imagine that I don't believe this to be true; but now it is clear to me that it really is true. I do think that the life of the Gods is everlasting, for this reason, because their joys are their own.[100] For immortality has been obtained by me, if no sorrow interrupts this delight. But whom in particular could I wish to be now thrown in my way, for me to relate these things to?

CHARINUS [Apart to himself]
What means this rapture?

PAMPHILUS [To himself]
I see Davus. There is no one in the world whom I would choose in preference; for I am sure that he of all people will sincerely rejoice in my happiness.

Enter **DAVUS**.

DAVUS [To himself]
Where is Pamphilus, I wonder?

PAMPHILUS
Here he is, Davus.

DAVUS [Turning round]
Who's that?

PAMPHILUS
'Tis I, Pamphilus; you don't know what has happened to me.

DAVUS
No really; but I know what has happened to myself.

PAMPHILUS
And I too.

DAVUS
It has fallen out just like human affairs in general, that you should know the mishap I have met with, before I the good that has befallen you.

PAMPHILUS
My Glycerium has discovered her parents.

DAVUS
O, well done!

CHARINUS [Apart, in surprise]
Hah!

PAMPHILUS
Her father is an intimate friend of ours.

DAVUS
Who?

PAMPHILUS
Chremes.

DAVUS
You do tell good news.

PAMPHILUS
And there's no hinderance to my marrying her at once.

CHARINUS [Apart]
Is he dreaming the same that he has been wishing for when awake?

PAMPHILUS
Then about the child, Davus.

DAVUS
O, say no more; you are the only person whom the Gods favor.

CHARINUS [Apart]
I'm all right if these things are true. I'll accost them.

[Comes forward.

PAMPHILUS
Who is this? Why, Charinus, you meet me at the very nick of time.

CHARINUS
That's all right.

PAMPHILUS
Have you heard—?

CHARINUS
Every thing; come, in your good fortune do have some regard for me. Chremes is now at your command; I'm sure that he'll do every thing you wish.

PAMPHILUS
I'll remember you; and because it is tedious for us to wait for him until he comes out, follow me this way; he is now in-doors at the house of Glycerium; do you, Davus, go home; send with all haste to remove her thence. Why are you standing there? Why are you delaying?

DAVUS
I'm going.

[**PAMPHILUS** and **CHARINUS** go into the house of **GLYCERIUM**. **DAVUS** then comes forward and addresses the Audience.

Don't you wait until they come out from there; she will be betrothed within: if there is any thing else that remains, it will be transacted in-doors. Grant us your applause.[101]

FOOTNOTES

[Footnote 1: From σιμὸς, "flat-nosed."]

[Footnote 2: From πᾶν, "all," and φιλὸς, "a friend."]

[Footnote 3: From σώζω, "to save;" saved in war.]

[Footnote 4: From χρέμπτομαι, "to spit."]

[Footnote 5: From ξάρις, "grace."]

[Footnote 6: From κριτής, "a judge."]

[Footnote 7: From Dacia, his native country; the Davi and Daci being the same people.]

[Footnote 8: From δρόμος, "a race."]

[Footnote 9: From πυῤῥὸς, "red-haired."]

[Footnote 10: From γλυκερὸς, "sweet."]

[Footnote 11: From Mysia, her native country.]

[Footnote 12: From Lesbos, her native country.]

[Footnote 13: The Megalensian Games]—These games were instituted at Rome in honor of the Goddess Cybele, when her statue was brought thither from Pessinum, in Asia Minor, by Scipio Nasica; they were so called from the Greek title Μεγάλη Μήτηρ, "the Great Mother." They were called Megalesia or Megalensia, indifferently. A very interesting account of the origin of these games will be found in the Fasti of Ovid. B. iv. l. 194, et seq.]

[Footnote 14: Being Curule Ædiles]—Among the other offices of the Ædiles at Rome, it was their duty to preside at the public games, and to provide the necessary dramatic representations for the Theatre, by making contracts with the Poets and Actors.]

[Footnote 15: Ambivius Turpio and Lucius Atilius Prænestinus]—These persons were the heads or managers of the company of actors who performed the Play, and as such it was their province to make the necessary contracts with the Curule Ædiles. They were also actors themselves, and usually took the leading characters. Ambivius Turpio seems to have been a favorite with the Roman public, and to have performed for many years; of L. Atilius Prænestinus nothing is known.]

[Footnote 16: Freedman of Claudius]—According to some, the words, "Flaccus Claudi" mean "the son of Claudius." It is, however, more generally thought that it is thereby meant that he was the freedman or liberated slave of some Roman noble of the family of the Claudii.]

[Footnote 17: Treble flutes and bass flutes]—The history of ancient music, and especially that relative to the "tibiæ," "pipes" or "flutes," is replete with obscurity. It is not agreed what are the meanings of the respective terms, but in the present Translation the following theory has been adopted: The words "dextræ" and "sinistræ" denote the kind of flute, the former being treble, the latter bass flutes, or, as they were sometimes called, "incentivæ" or "succentivæ;" though it has been thought by some that they were so called because the former held with the right hand, the latter with the left. When two treble flutes or two bass flutes were played upon at the same time, they were called "tibiæ pares;" but when one was "dextra" and the other "sinistra," "tibiæ impares." Hence the words "paribus dextris et sinistris," would mean alternately with treble flutes and bass flutes. Two "tibiæ" were often played upon by one performer at the same time. For a specimen of a Roman "tibicen" or "piper," see the last scene of the Stichus of Plautus. Some curious information relative to the pipers of Rome and the legislative enactments respecting them will be found in the Fasti of Ovid, B. vi. l. 653, et seq.]

[Footnote 18: It is entirety Grecian]—This means that the scene is in Greece, and that it is of the kind called "palliata," as representing the manners of the Greeks, who wore the "pallium," or outer cloak; whereas the Romans wore the "toga." In the Prologue, Terence states that he borrowed it from the Greek of Menander.]

[Footnote 19: Being Consuls]—M. Claudius Marcellus and C. Sulpicius Galba were Consuls in the year from the building of Rome 586, and B.C. 167.]

[Footnote 20: A malevolent old Poet]—Ver. 7. He alludes to Luscus Lanuvinus, or Lavinius, a Comic Poet of his time, but considerably his senior. He is mentioned by Terence in all his Prologues except that to the Hecyra, and seems to have made it the business of his life to run down his productions and discover faults in them.]

[Footnote 21: Composed the Andrian]—Ver. 9. This Play, like that of our author, took its name from the Isle of Andros, one of the Cyclades in the Ægean Sea, where Glycerium is supposed to have been born. Donatus, the Commentator on Terence, informs us that the first Scene of this Play is almost a literal translation from the Perinthian of Menander, in which the old man was represented as discoursing with his wife just as Simo does here with Sosia. In the Andrian of Menander, the old man opened with a soliloquy.]

[Footnote 22: And the Perinthian]—Ver. 9. This Play was so called from Perinthus, a town of Thrace, its heroine being a native of that place.]

[Footnote 23: Nævius, Plautus, and Ennius]—Ver. 18. Ennius was the oldest of these three Poets. Nævius a contemporary of Plautus. See a probable allusion to his misfortunes in the Miles Gloriosus of Plautus, l. 211.]

[Footnote 24: The mystifying carefulness]—Ver. 21. By "obscuram diligentiam" he means that formal degree of precision which is productive of obscurity.]

[Footnote 25: Are to be taken care of, I suppose]—Ver. 30. "Nempe ut curentur recte hæc." Colman here remarks; "Madame Dacier will have it that Simo here makes use of a kitchen term in the word 'curentur.' I believe it rather means 'to take care of' any thing generally; and at the conclusion of this very scene, Sosia uses the word again, speaking of things very foreign to cookery, 'Sat est, curabo.'"]

[Footnote 26: To be my freedman]—Ver. 37. "Libertus" was the name given to a slave set at liberty by his master. A "libertinus" was the son of a "libertus."]

[Footnote 27: As it were a censure]—Ver. 43. Among the Greeks (whose manners and sentiments are supposed to be depicted in this Play) it was a maxim that he who did a kindness should forget it, while he who received it should keep it in memory. Sosia consequently feels uneasy, and considers the remark of his master in the light of a reproach.]

[Footnote 28: After he had passed from youthfulness]—Ver. 51. "Ephebus" was the name given to a youth when between the ages of sixteen and twenty.]

[Footnote 29: And a master]—Ver. 54. See the Notes to the Translation of the Bacchides of Plautus, l. 109, where Lydus, a slave, appears as the "pædagogus," or "magister," of Pistoclerus.]

[Footnote 30: Or to the philosophers]—Ver. 57. It was the custom in Greece with all young men of free birth to apply themselves to the study of philosophy, of course with zeal proportioned to the love of learning in each. They each adopted some particular sect, to which they attached themselves. There is something sarcastic here, and indeed not very respectful to the "philosophers," in coupling them as objects of attraction with horses and hounds.]

[Footnote 31: Nothing to excess]—Ver. 61. "Ne quid nimis." This was one of the three sentences which were inscribed in golden letters in the Temple of Apollo at Delphi. The two others were "Know thyself," and "Misery is the consequence of debt and discord." Sosia seems from the short glimpse we have of him to have been a retailer of old saws and proverbs. He is unfortunately only a Protatic or introductory character, as we lose sight of him after this Act.]

[Footnote 32: Meanwhile, three years ago]—Ver. 60. The following remark of Donatus on this passage is quoted by Colman for its curiosity. "The Author has artfully said three years, when he might have given a longer or a shorter period; since it is probable that the woman might have lived modestly one year; set up the trade the next; and died the third. In the first year, therefore, Pamphilus knew nothing of the family of Chrysis; in the second, he became acquainted with Glycerium; and in the third, Glycerium marries Pamphilus, and finds her parents."]

[Footnote 33: He is smitten]—Ver. 78. "Habet," literally "He has it." This was the expression used by the spectators at the moment when a Gladiator was wounded by his antagonist. In the previous line, in the words "captus est," a figurative allusion is made to the "retiarius," a Gladiator who was provided with a net, with which he endeavored to entangle his opponent.]

[Footnote 34: Gave his contribution]—Ver. 88. "Symbolam." The "symbolæ," "shot" at picnic or club entertainments, are more than once alluded to in the Notes to the Translation of Plautus.]

[Footnote 35: Even I myself]—Ver. 116. Cooke remarks here: "A complaisant father, to go to the funeral of a courtesan, merely to oblige his son!"]

[Footnote 36: The female attendants]—Ver. 123. "Pedissequæ." These "pedissequæ," or female attendants, are frequently alluded to in the Plays of Plautus. See the Notes to Bohn's Translation.]

[Footnote 37: To the burying-place]—Ver. 128. "Sepulcrum" strictly means, the tomb or place for burial, but here the funeral pile itself. When the bones were afterward buried on the spot where they were burned, it was called "bustum."]

[Footnote 38: Troubles itself about that]—Ver. 185. He says this contemptuously, as if it was likely that the public should take any such great interest in his son as the father would imply by his remark. By thus saying, he also avoids giving a direct reply.]

[Footnote 39: Davus, not Œdipus]—Ver. 194. Alluding to the circumstance of Œdipus alone being able to solve the riddle of the Sphynx.]

[Footnote 40: To the mill]—Ver. 199. The "pistrinum," or "hand-mill," for grinding corn, was used as a mode of punishment for refractory slaves. See the Notes to the Translation of Plautus.]

[Footnote 41: Those in their dotage, not those who dote in love]—Ver. 218. There is a jingle intended in this line, in the resemblance between "amentium," "mad persons," and "amantium," "lovers."]

[Footnote 42: They have resolved to rear]—Ver. 219. This passage alludes to the custom among the Greeks of laying new-born children on the ground, upon which the father, or other person who undertook the care of the child, lifted it from the ground, "tollebat." In case no one took charge of the child, it was exposed, which was very frequently done in the case of female children. Plato was the first to inveigh against this barbarous practice. It is frequently alluded to in the Plays of Plautus.]

[Footnote 43: Hence to the Forum]—Ver. 226. Colman has the following remark: "The Forum is frequently spoken of in the Comic Authors; and from various passages in which Terence mentions it, it may be collected that it was a public place, serving the several purposes of a market, the seat of the courts of justice, a public walk, and an exchange."]

[Footnote 44: Wine-bibbing]—Ver. 229. The nurses and midwives of antiquity seem to have been famed for their tippling propensities. In some of the Plays of Plautus we do not find them spared.]

[Footnote 45: Rearing some monster]—Ver. 250. "Aliquid monstri alunt." Madame Dacier and some other Commentators give these words the rather far-fetched meaning of "They are hatching some plot." Donatus, with much more probability, supposes him to refer to the daughter of Chremes, whom, as the young women among the Greeks were brought up in great seclusion, we may suppose Pamphilus never to have seen.]

[Footnote 46: She is oppressed with grief]—Ver. 268. "Laborat a dolore." Colman has the following remark upon this passage: "Though the word 'laborat' has tempted Donatus and the rest of the Commentators to suppose that this sentence signifies Glycerium being in labor, I can not help concurring with Cooke, that it means simply that she is weighed down with grief. The words immediately subsequent corroborate this interpretation; and at the conclusion of the Scene, when Mysis tells him that she is going for a midwife, Pamphilus hurries her away, as he would naturally have done here had he understood by these words that her mistress was in labor."]

[Footnote 47: By your good Genius]—Ver. 289. "Per Genium tuum." This was a common expression with the Romans, and is used by Horace, Epistles, B. i., Ep. 7:—

"Quod te per Genium dextramque Deosque Penates,
Obsecro, et obtestor—"

The word "Genius" signified the tutelary God who was supposed to attend every person from the period of his birth. The signification of the word will be found further referred to in the Notes to the Translation of Plautus.]

[Footnote 48: To fetch the midwife]—Ver. 299. Cooke has the following remark here: "Methinks Mysis has loitered a little too much, considering the business which she was sent about; but perhaps Terence knew that some women were of such a temper as to gossip on the way, though an affair of life or death requires their haste." Colman thus takes him to task for this observation: "This two-edged reflection, glancing at once on Terence and the ladies, is, I think, very ill-founded. The delay of Mysis, on seeing the emotion of Pamphilus, is very natural; and her artful endeavors to interest Pamphilus on behalf of her mistress, are rather marks of her attention than neglect."]

[Footnote 49: Charinus and Byrrhia]. We learn from Donatus that the characters of Charinus and Byrrhia were not introduced in the work of Menander, but were added to the Play of Terence, lest Philumena's being left without a husband, on the marriage of Pamphilus to Glycerium, should appear too tragical a circumstance. Diderot is of opinion that Terence did not improve his Play by this addition.]

[Footnote 50: Tell me nothing]—Ver. 336. It has been suggested that this refers to Byrrhia's dissuading his master from addressing Pamphilus, or else to what he has told him concerning the intended marriage. Westerhovius thinks that Byrrhia is just then whispering some trifling nonsense in his master's ear, which he, occupied with more important cares, is unwilling to attend to.]

[Footnote 51: To a high place]—Ver. 356. He probably alludes to some part of the Acropolis, the citadel, or higher part of Athens, which commanded a view of the lower town.]

[Footnote 52: Stillness before the door]—Ver. 362. Madame Dacier observes that this remark is very appropriately made by Davus, as showing that the marriage was clearly not intended by Chremes. The house of the bride on such an occasion would be thronged by her friends, and at the door would be the musicians and those who were to form part of the bridal procession.]

[Footnote 53: No matron at the house]—Ver. 364. By the use of the word "matrona," he probably alludes to the "pronubæ" among the Romans, whose duties were somewhat similar to those of our bride's-maids. At the completion of the bridal repast, the bride was conducted to the bridal chamber by matrons who had not had more than one husband.]

[Footnote 54: An obol's worth]—Ver. 369. The "obelus" was the smallest Greek silver coin, and was equal in value to about three halfpence of our money. "Pisciculi minuti," "little fish," were much used for food among the poorer classes; "mena," a fish resembling our pilchard, was a common article of food with the Romans. The larger kinds of fish went under the general name of "cetum."]

[Footnote 55: I have now followed him]—Ver. 414. "Hunc venientem sequor." Cooke has the following remark on this line: "This verse, though in every edition, as Bentley judiciously observes, is certainly spurious; for as Pamphilus has not disappeared since Byrrhia left the stage, he could not say 'nunc hunc venientem sequor.' If we suppose the line genuine, we must at the same time suppose Terence guilty of a monstrous absurdity." On these words Colman makes the following just observations: "Other Commentators have also stumbled at this passage; but if in the words 'followed him hither,' we suppose 'him' (hunc) to refer to Simo, the difficulty is removed; and that the pronoun really does signify Simo, is evident from the circumstance of Pamphilus never having left the stage since the disappearance of

Byrrhia. Simo is also represented as coming on the stage homeward, so that Byrrhia might easily have followed him along the street; and it is evident that Byrrhia does not allude to Pamphilus from the agreeable surprise which he expresses on seeing him there so opportunely for the purpose."]

[Footnote 56: Inflict evil upon me]—Ver. 431. "Malum;" the usual name by which slaves spoke of the beatings they were in the habit of receiving at the hands or by the order of their irascible masters. Colman has the following remarks: "Donatus observes on this Scene between Byrrhia, Simo, Pamphilus, and Davus, that the dialogue is sustained by four persons, who have little or no intercourse with each other; so that the Scene is not only in direct contradiction to the precept of Horace, excluding a fourth person, but is also otherwise vicious in its construction. Scenes of this kind are, I think, much too frequent in Terence, though, indeed, the form of the ancient Theatre was more adapted to the representation of them than the modern. The multiplicity of speeches aside is also the chief error in this dialogue; such speeches, though very common in dramatic writers, ancient and modern, being always more or less unnatural."]

[Footnote 57: What does he say, Davus?]—Ver. 434. "Quid, Dave, narrat?" This reading Vollbehr suggests in place of the old one, "Quid Davus narrat?" and upon good grounds, as it appears. According to the latter reading we are to suppose that Davus is grumbling to himself, on which Simo says, "What does Davus say?" It seems, however, much more likely that Davus accompanies Pamphilus to the door, and speaks to him before he goes in, and then, on his return to Simo, the latter asks him, "What does he say, Davus?"]

[Footnote 58: Just as much as nothing]—Ver. 434. "Æque quidquam nunc quidem." This is a circumlocution for "nothing at all:" somewhat more literally perhaps, it might be rendered "just as much as before." Perizonius supplies the ellipsis with a long string of Latin words, which translated would mean, "Now, indeed, he says equally as much as he says then, when he says nothing at all."]

[Footnote 59: Amount of ten drachmæ]—Ver. 451. The Attic drachma was a silver coin worth in value about 9¾d. of English money.]

[Footnote 60: Juno Lucina]—Ver. 473. Juno Lucina had the care of women in childbed. Under this name some suppose Diana to have been worshiped. A similar incident to the present is found in the Adelphi, l. 486; and in the Aulularia of Plautus, l. 646.]

[Footnote 61: Are your scholars forgetful?]—Ver. 477. He alludes under this term to Mysis, Lesbia, and Pamphilus, whom he supposes Davus to have been training to act their parts in the plot against him.]

[Footnote 62: Let her bathe]—Ver. 483. It was the custom for women to bathe immediately after childbirth. See the Amphitryon of Plautus, l. 669, and the Note to the passage in Bohn's Translation.]

[Footnote 63: Be laying the child]—Ver. 507. Colman has the following remark on this line:—"The art of this passage is equal to the pleasantry, for though Davus runs into this detail merely with a view to dupe the old man still further by flattering him on his fancied sagacity, yet it very naturally prepares us for an incident which, by another turn of circumstances, afterward becomes necessary."]

[Footnote 64: Proved to be false]—Ver. 513. That is, according to Simo's own notion, which Davus now thinks proper to humor.]

[Footnote 65: To Bring a child at the same time]—Ver. 515. This is a piece of roguery which has probably been practiced in all ages, and was somewhat commonly perpetrated in Greece. The reader of English history will remember how the unfortunate son of James II was said, in the face of the strongest evidence to the contrary, to have been a supposititious child brought into the queen's chamber in a silver warming-pan.]

[Footnote 66: But I do not think]—Ver. 563-4. "At ego non posse arbitror neque illum hane perpetuo habere." Chremes uses an ambiguous expression here, perhaps purposely. It may mean, "I do not think that he can possibly be constant to her," or, "that she will continue to live with him."]

[Footnote 67: A sure son-in-law]—Ver. 571. By the use of the word "firmum," he means a son-in-law who will not be likely to resort to divorce or separation from his wife.]

[Footnote 68: Why isn't the bride sent for?]—Ver. 582. Among the Greeks the bride was conducted by the bridegroom at nightfall from her father's house, in a chariot drawn by a pair of mules or oxen, and escorted by persons carrying the nuptial torches. Among the Romans she proceeded in the evening to the bridegroom's house; preceded by a boy carrying a torch of white thorn, or, according to some, of pine-wood. To this custom reference is indirectly made in the present passage.]

[Footnote 69: I myself, indeed!]—Ver. 597. No doubt Davus says these words in sorrow and regret; Simo, however, supposes them to be uttered in exultation at the apparent success of his plans. Consequently "vero" is intended by Davus to have the sense here of "too truly."]

[Footnote 70: To a frivolous slave]—Ver. 610. "Servo futili." According to the Scholiast on the Thebais of Statius, B. viii. l. 297, "vas futile" was a kind of vessel with a broad mouth and narrow bottom, used in the rites of Vesta. It was made of that peculiar shape in order that the priest should be obliged to hold it during the sacrifices, and might not set it on the ground, which was considered profane; as, if set there, the contents must necessarily fall out. From this circumstance, men who could not contain a secret were sometimes called "futiles."]

[Footnote 71: You scoundrel]—Ver. 619. "Furcifer;" literally, wearer of the "furca," or wooden collar. This method of punishment has been referred to in the Notes to the Translation of Plautus.]

[Footnote 72: What do you deserve?]—Ver. 622. Madame Dacier remarks that this question is taken from the custom of the Athenians, who never condemned a criminal without first asking him what punishment he thought he deserved; and according to the nature of his answer they mitigated or increased his punishment. Tho Commentators quote a similar passage from the Frogs of Aristophanes.]

[Footnote 73: The cross]—Ver. 622. The "cross," "crux," as a punishment for refractory slaves has been remarked upon in the Notes to the Translation of Plautus.]

[Footnote 74: The circumstances]—Ver. 635. "Res." According, however, to Donatus, this word has the meaning here of "malice" or "spitefulness."]

[Footnote 75: Concerned in my own interests]—Ver. 637. Equivalent to our sayings, "Charity begins at home;" "Take care of number one."]

[Footnote 76: They are not ashamed]—Ver. 638. Terence has probably borrowed this remark from the Epidicus of Plautus, l. 165-6: "Generally all men are ashamed when it is of no use; when they ought to be ashamed, then does shame forsake them, when occasion is for them to be ashamed."]

[Footnote 77: Makes a noise]—Ver. 683. The doors with the Romans opened inwardly, while those of the Greeks opened on the outside. It was therefore usual with them, when coming out, to strike the door on the inside with a stick or with the knuckles, that those outside might be warned to get out of the way. Patrick, however, observes with some justice, that the word "concrepuit" may here allude to the creaking of the hinges. See the Curculio of Plautus, l. 160, where the Procuress pours water on the hinges, in order that Cappadox may not hear the opening of the door.]

[Footnote 78: Take some sacred herbs]—Ver. 727. "Verbena" appears to have been a general term applied to any kind of herb used in honor of the Deities, or to the boughs and leaves of any tree gathered from a pure or sacred place. Fresh "verbenæ" were placed upon the altars every day. See the Mercator of Plautus, l. 672.]

[Footnote 79: From the altar here]—Ver. 727. It was usual to have altars on the stage; when Comedy was performed, one on the left hand in honor of Apollo, and on the representation of Tragedy, one on the right in honor of Bacchus. It has been suggested that Terence here alludes to the former of these. As, however, at Athens almost every house had its own altar in honor of Apollo Prostaterius just outside of the street door, it is most probable that to one of these altars reference is here made. They are frequently alluded to in the Plays of Plautus.]

[Footnote 80: Which I had first purposed, I now give up]—Ver. 734. His first intention no doubt was to go and inform Simo of the child being laid at the door.]

[Footnote 81: Whenever there's necessity]—Ver. 737. He retires without fully explaining his intention to Mysis; consequently, in the next Scene she gives an answer to Chremes which Davus does not intend.]

[Footnote 82: Stuffed out beneath her clothes]—Ver. 771. "Suffarcinatam." He alludes to the trick already referred to as common among the Greeks, of the nurses and midwives secretly introducing supposititious children; see l. 515 and the Note.]

[Footnote 83: Several free women were present]—Ver. 772. She speaks of "liberæ," "free women," because in Greece as well as Italy slaves were not permitted to give evidence. See the Curculio of Plautus, l. 621, and the Note to the passage in Bohn's Translation. See also the remark of Geta in the Phormio, l. 293.]

[Footnote 84: Constrained by the laws]—Ver. 782. He alludes to a law at Athens which compelled a man who had debauched a free-born woman to marry her. This is said by Davus with the view of frightening Chremes from the match.]

[Footnote 85: She ought to be carried off]—Ver. 787. He says this implying that Mysis, who is a slave, ought to be put to the torture to confess the truth; as it was the usual method at Athens to force a confession from slaves by that method. We find in the Hecyra, Bacchis readily offering her slaves to be put to the torture, and in the Adelphi the same custom is alluded to in the scene between Micio, Hegio, and Geta.]

[Footnote 86: Descended to me by law]—Ver. 800. On the supposition that Chrysis died without a will, Crito as her next of kin would be entitled to her effects.]

[Footnote 87: Is Chrysis then—?]—Ver. 804. This is an instance of Aposiopesis; Crito, much affected, is unwilling to name the death of Chrysis. It was deemed of ill omen to mention death, and numerous Euphemisms or circumlocutions were employed in order to avoid the necessity of doing so.]

[Footnote 88: Warn me, a stranger]—Ver. 812. Patrick has the following remarks upon this passage: "Madame Dacier observes that it appears, from Xenophon's Treatise on the policy of the Athenians, that all the inhabitants of cities and islands in alliance with Athens were obliged in all claims to repair thither, and refer their cause to the decision of the people, not being permitted to plead elsewhere. We can not wonder then that Crito is unwilling to engage in a suit so inconvenient from its length, expense, and little prospect of success." She might have added that such was the partiality and corruptness of the Athenian people, that, being a stranger, his chances of success would probably be materially diminished.]

[Footnote 89: You set in motion]—Ver. 865. By the use of the word "Commotus" he seems to allude to the wretched, restless existence of a man tied hand and foot, and continually working at the hand-mill. Westerhovius thinks that Simo uses this word sarcastically, in allusion to the words of Davus, at the beginning of the present Scene, "Animo otioso esse impero;" "I bid you set your minds at ease."]

[Footnote 90: Hands and feet together]—Ver. 866. "Quadrupedem." Literally "as a quadruped" or "all fours." Echard remarks that it was the custom of the Athenians to tie criminals hands and feet together, just like calves.]

[Footnote 91: Without regard to the custom and the law]—Ver. 880. There was a law among the Athenians which forbade citizens to marry strangers, and made the offspring of such alliances illegitimate; the same law also excluded such as were not born of two citizens from all offices of trust and honor.]

[Footnote 92: Could opportunely suggest to him]—Ver. 919. Colman has the following remark on this line: "Madame Dacier and several English Translators make Pamphilus say that he could give Crito a hint or two. What hints he could propose to suggest to Crito, I can not conceive. The Italian translation, printed with the Vatican Terence, seems to understand the words in the same manner that I have translated them, in which sense (the pronoun 'illum' referring to Simo instead of Crito) they seem to be the most natural words of Pamphilus on occasion of his father's anger and the speech immediately preceding."]

[Footnote 93: A sharper]—Ver. 920. "Sycophanta." For some account of the "sycophantæ," "swindlers" or "sharpers" of ancient times, see the Notes to the Trinummus of Plautus, Bohn's Translation.]

[Footnote 94: A long time ago]—Ver. 924. The story begins with "Olim," just in the same way that with us nursery tales commence with "There was, a long time ago."]

[Footnote 95: A citizen of Rhamnus]—Ver. 931. Rhamnus was a maritime town of Attica, near which many of the more wealthy Athenians had country-seats. It was famous for the Temple of Nemesis there, the Goddess of Vengeance, who was thence called "Rhamnusia." In this Temple was her statue, carved by Phidias out of the marble which the Persians brought to Greece for the purpose of making a statue of

Victory out of it, and which was thus appropriately devoted to the Goddess of Retribution. The statue wore a crown, and had wings, and, holding a spear of ash in the right hand, it was seated on a stag.]

[Footnote 96: One difficulty]—Ver. 941. "Scrupus," or "scrupulus," was properly a stone or small piece of gravel which, getting into the shoe, hurt the foot; hence the word figuratively came to mean a "scruple," "difficulty," or "doubt." We have a similar expression: "to be graveled."]

[Footnote 97: A knot in a bulrush]—Ver. 942. "Nodum in scirpo quærere" was a proverbial expression implying a desire to create doubts and difficulties where there really were none; there being no knots in the bulrush. The same expression occurs in the Menæchmi of Plautus, l. 247.]

[Footnote 98: Of course—Then be it so]—Ver. 951. "Nempe id. Scilicet." Colman has the following remark on this line: "Donatus, and some others after him, understand these words of Simo and Pamphilus as requiring a fortune of Chremes with his daughter; and one of them says that Simo, in order to explain his meaning, in the representation, should produce a bag of money. This surely is precious refinement, worthy the genius of a true Commentator. Madame Dacier, who entertains a just veneration for Donatus, doubts the authenticity of the observation ascribed to him. The sense I have followed is, I think, the most obvious and natural interpretation of the words of Pamphilus and Simo, which refers to the preceding, not the subsequent, speech of Chremes."]

[Footnote 99: He is not rightly bound]—Ver. 956. "Non recte vinctus;" meaning "it was not well done to bind him." The father pretends to understand him as meaning (which he might equally well by using the same words), "non satis stricte," "he wasn't tightly enough" bound; and answers "I ordered that he should be," referring to his order for Davus to be bound hand and foot. Donatus justly observes that the disposition of the old gentleman to joke is a characteristic mark of his thorough reconciliation.]

[Footnote 100: Their joys are their own]—Ver. 961. Westorhovius remarks that he seems here to be promulgating the doctrine of Epicurus, who taught that the Deities devoted themselves entirely to pleasure and did not trouble themselves about mortals. Donatas observes that these are the doctrines of Epicurus and that the whole sentence is copied from the Eunuch of Menander; to which practice of borrowing from various Plays, allusion is made in the Prologue, where he mentions the mixing of plays; "contaminari fabulas."]

[Footnote 101: Grant us your applause]—Ver. 982. "Plaudite." Colman has the following remark at the conclusion of this Play: "All the old Tragedies and Comedies acted at Rome concluded in this manner. 'Donec cantor vos "Plaudite" dicat,' says Horace. Who the 'cantor' was, is a matter of dispute. Madame Dacier thinks it was the whole chorus; others suppose it to have been a single actor; some the prompter, and some the composer. Before the word 'Plaudite' in all the old copies is an Ω which has also given rise to several learned conjectures. It is most probable, according to the notion of Madame Dacier, that this Ω, being the last letter of the Greek alphabet, was nothing more than the mark of the transcriber to signify the end, like the Latin word 'Finis' in modern books; or it might, as Patrick supposes, stand for Ωδος, 'cantor,' denoting that the following word 'Plaudite' was spoken by him. After 'Plaudite' in all the old copies of Terence stand these two words, 'Calliopius recensui;' which signify, 'I, Calliopius, have revised and corrected this piece.' And this proceeds from the custom of the old critics, who carefully revised all Manuscripts, and when they had read and corrected any work, certified the same by placing their names at the end of it."]

Henry Thomas Riley (Translator)

Riley was born in June 1816, the only son of Henry Riley of Southwark, an ironmonger.

He was educated at Chatham House, Ramsgate, and at Charterhouse School. University was at Trinity College, Cambridge, but at the end of his first term he moved to Clare College where he was admitted on 17th December 1834 and elected a scholar on 24th January 1835.

He graduated B.A. in 1840.

Riley was called to the bar at the Inner Temple on 23rd November 1847, but early in life he worked for booksellers, editing and translating. These skills were to bring him perhaps the real jewels of his legacy with his translations of Terence, Ovid, Plautus and Lucan during the 1850's.

When the Royal Charter of April 1869 set up the Historical Manuscripts Commission he was engaged as an inspector and tasked with examining the archives of various municipal corporations, the muniments of the colleges at Oxford and Cambridge, and the documents in the registries of various bishops and chapters.

Henry Thomas Riley died at Hainault House, the Crescent, Selhurst, Croydon, on 14th April 1878, aged 61.

Terence – A Concise Bibliography

Andria (The Girl from Andros) (166 BC)
Hecyra (The Mother-in-Law) (165 BC)
Heauton Timorumenos (The Self-Tormentor) (163 BC)
Phormio (The Scheming Parasite) (161 BC)
Eunuchus (The Eunuch) (161 BC)
Adelphoe (The Brothers) (160 BC)

The first known printed edition of Terence appeared in Strasbourg in 1470.